T0208016

PURPOSELY LIVING A BLESSED LIFE THROUGH THE MIND, THE HEART & THE MOUTH

Vernadette Augustusel

WESTBOW
PRESS®
A DIVISION OF THOMAS NELSON
& ZONDERVAN

WestBow Press books may be ordered through booksellers or by contacting:

WestBow Press
A Division of Thomas Nelson & Zondervan
1663 Liberty Drive
Bloomington, IN 47403
www.westbowpress.com
844-714-3454

ISBN: 978-1-6642-7347-4 (sc)
ISBN: 978-1-6642-7346-7 (e)

Library of Congress Control Number: 2022913596

Print information available on the last page.

WestBow Press rev. date: 8/16/2022

CONTENTS

Acknowledgments ix

Introduction xi

Chapter 1   Possessing the Blessings of the Kingdom:
             What Is the Kingdom, and Where Is It? 1
Chapter 2   Terms of the Covenant: A Covenant Connection 19
Chapter 3   Taking a Closer Look 31
Chapter 4   A Perfect Example 38
Chapter 5   The Mind: What's on Your Mind? 46
Chapter 6   The Heart: What's in Your Heart? 53
Chapter 7   The Mouth: What Is Coming Out of Your Mouth? 60
Chapter 8   God's Promises: A Divine Assurance of a
             Blessed Life 80

Prayer and Instruction for a Redeemed Life 89
Prayer of Agreement 91
Bibliography 93

ACKNOWLEDGMENTS

In honor of my husband, Elder Nathaniel Augustusel, who

helped, encouraged, and believed in me to pursue my

dreams and calling. To the countless church members,

friends, and family, stay blessed, and continue to be

a blessing to me and each other.

INTRODUCTION

In the Beginning, the Word

Living a Blessed Life through the Mind, the Heart, and the Mouth begins by applying the Word of God to our minds and sowing it in our hearts by speaking it out of our mouths. If one were to study and reflect on the Word of God, the individual would soon come to know, learn, and understand that it is full of promises to live a blessed life. With the Word of God in our hearts, on our minds, and spoken out of our mouths, we will live and possess a blessed life, a life that is fulfilled. The Word reassures us that if we do what it says, we will live an abundant life. Jesus said that "The thief comes only in order to steal and kill and destroy. I came that they may have life, and have it in abundance [to the full, till it overflows]" (John 10:10 AMP). Take Joshua 1:7–8 (AMP), for example. It says, "Be strong and very courageous, be careful to obey all the law (the word) my servant Moses gave you; do not turn from it to the right or to the left, that you may be successful wherever you go. Do not let this 'Book of the Law,' the word depart from your mouth; meditate on it day and night, so you will be prosperous and successful." In other words, for one to be prosperous and to live a successful life means to have an abundant life, a blessed life. Not only does Joshua 1:7–8 tell us what and how to meditate on the Word of God, but when to meditate on it—day and night.

Most of us understand and associate the art of meditating with Eastern religions and practices. One well-known form of meditation involves chanting statements of their beliefs while relaxing and being tranquil and calm. But believe it or not, Christians are the ones who should be meditating on the Word of God as it is stated in Joshua 1:8. The term "meditate" here means to ponder and mutter God's Word. To ponder a thing means to think and concentrate on something over and over again. Now, to mutter something, is slightly different. It means to say something, key words, softly over and over to oneself. "Day" and "night" we know are terms that refer to time, but I believe metaphorically, they also symbolize something else here. The term "day" can also mean or represent youth and new beginnings. The scripture would then mean we should study, ponder, and mutter the Word during our youth or in the new beginning of new life experiences. Night does not always mean in the evening time. It can also symbolize adversity, trouble, wickedness, late adulthood (like the elderly), and/or evil. The scripture would then mean that we need to meditate on the Word of God when facing life troubles, challenges, and uncertainties.

James 1:16–21 (ASV) tells us,

> Do not be deceived, my beloved brethren. Every good thing given, and every perfect gift is from above, coming down from the Father of lights, with whom there is no variation or shifting shadow. In the exercise of His will He brought us forth by the word of truth, so that we would be a kind of first fruits among His creatures. This you know, my beloved brethren. But everyone must be quick to hear, slow to speak and slow to anger; for the anger of man does not achieve the righteousness of God. Therefore,

putting aside all filthiness and all that remains of
wickedness, in humility receive the word implanted,
which is able to save your souls.

I love this portion of the Scriptures because God reminds us that
we are first loved, and that every good and perfect gift comes from
him, even the promises of a blessed life. Then the Word goes on to tell
us that God will not change, like so many things in life have or will
from one moment to the next. We live in a world that is constantly
changing. Sometimes we find ourselves having to adapt quickly and
being flexible to be able to flow and function in this life. However,
there are two points here I would like to draw attention to. The first
one is that God chose to give us birth through the word of truth, the
spoken word of truth. It is a blessing that God chose to rebirth—or
shall I say give us new lives—through his Word. Jesus himself said
that the Word is alive and active.

Let's examine in this book how God will birth or rebirth new
lives, blessed lives for us through the self-fulfilling power of his Word.
When the Word of God is humbly accepted in our minds, spoken
from our mouths, and sown in our hearts, a rebirthing process begins
in our lives. These three functions must operate with God's Word
to begin a blessed new life. To humbly accept the Word means to
accept the Word without reasoning, reservation, skepticism, or by
challenging it. Rather, we must fully trust in it. Accepting the Word
of God in our minds, hearts, and mouths is when we begin acting
like God intended us to when he created our world.

In Genesis chapters 1–2, we find the creation story of the earth,
man, and every animal. God said let there be. And it was and came
into existence. God responded to what he made by saying it was good.
Since we were created in God's image and likeness, he wants us to
experience and operate in the same creative power that he has given us
to live a blessed life. Without sounding all weird, we have the power
and authority to help create the world in which we live. Our world,

or better said, the atmosphere in which we live is blessed. If we allow it, the Word of God can help transform our lives from the inside out.

This scripture goes on to say that if we humbly accept the Word of God planted in us, we will be saved. The term "saved" here does not just mean the act of receiving the gift of salvation one time. It literally means to heal, preserve, deliver, protect, do well, and be made whole. In other words, it means to live a blessed life.

The Word of God has the power to set the course of one's life in the right direction, toward a prosperous and blessed life. Or it could go in the wrong direction, which would produce a damaged, meaningless and poor life. But God's desire is for us to have bountiful lives because blessed, bountiful lives glorify him and show him to be a good God. "Let them shout for joy and be glad, who favor my righteous cause; And let them say continually, 'Let the Lord be magnified, who has pleasure in the prosperity of His servant'" (Psalm 35:27 NKJV). God the Father wants, desires, and delights and takes pleasure in his children doing well and prospering.

However, the enemy comes with thoughts and ideas that you are nothing and will never have or be anything. But you don't have to agree with him. You know he came to destroy your life the same way God came to bless your life through your mind, your mouth, and your heart. God's Word, united with our faith, will produce a blessed life. However, worries of the world, the deceitfulness of riches, and the lust for other things can and will block, stop, and hinder a blessed life.

Remember, our heavenly Father want us to have good success, blessings. There is success, but then there's *good* success, which I believe is success with peace and enjoyment. After all, not all success is enjoyed with peace. However, when we neglect the seed of God's Word from being sown in our lives, we fail to live the best lives God has for us. In Mark 4:1–20 and Luke 8:11–15, it is made very clear in the parable Jesus taught about the seed of the Word being sown into your heart, your life. This is represented as four types of soil. The seed is the Word of God. Those along the path are the ones who hear the Word, and immediately, the devil comes and takes away the Word that was sown in their hearts so that they may not believe and be saved. Those seeds that fell on the rocks have no roots, and they are the ones who receive the Word with joy when they hear it. They believe for a while, but in the time of testing, they fall away from the truth and away from God because they have no roots. Seeds that fell among thorns stand for those who hear, but as soon as they go on their way, they are choked by life's worries, by the riches and pleasures of life. The Word is then choked out of them, and they do not mature to possess the promised blessed life.

We must acknowledge that seeds—the Word—sown in good soil represent those with noble and good hearts who hear the Word, retain the Word, and persevere in the Word to produce a crop of good fruit, which is evidence of a blessed life. In other words, to produce a crop means to have something you never had before, to increase blessings spiritually, mentally, physically, and materially. Since we are three-part beings, we are spiritual beings who live in a body and possess a soul. We have needs, desires, and wants for every aspect of our lives. We can experience and have increased blessings in every part of our lives through the Word.

> Again, Jesus began to teach beside the sea [of Galilee].
> And a very large crowd gathered around Him, so He
> got into a boat [anchoring it a short distance out]
> on the sea and sat down; and the whole crowd was
> by the sea on the shore. And He taught them many
> things in parables, and in His teaching, He said to
> them, "Listen! A Sower went out to sow seed; and as
> he was sowing, some seed fell by the road; and the
> birds came and ate it up. Other seed fell on rocks
> where there was not much soil; and immediately a
> plant sprang up because the soil had no depth. And
> when the sun came up, the plant was scorched; and

because it had no root, it dried up and withered away. Other seed fell among thorns, and the thorns came up and choked it, and it yielded no grain. And other seed fell into good soil, and as the plants grew and increased, they yielded a crop and produced thirty, sixty, and a hundred times [as much as had been sown]." And He said, "He who has ears to hear, let him hear and heed My words." (Mark 4:1–9 AMP)

CHAPTER 1

*Possessing the Blessings of the Kingdom:
What Is the Kingdom, and Where Is It?*

Genesis 1:26–27; 2:27
Numbers 23:19
Daniel 6:26
Isaiah 55:8–9

Psalms 51:10; 119:11
Matthew 6:1, 33
Mark 10:29–30; 11:11; 12:13–17; 16:19
Luke 17:20–21; 22:35–38
John 1:1, 12–13; 10:10; 14:2–3; 14:4–6
Acts 1:3–7
Romans 8:6–16; 12:2; 14:17, 26–28
1 Corinthians 15:45–50
2 Corinthians 3:2; 5:1–10
Ephesians 2:11–21
Philippians 3:17–20
1 Thessalonians 5:23

2 Timothy 2:7
Titus 3:1–7
Hebrews 6:6
James 5:16–17
1 John 4:8
3 John 1:2

God's Will

It is most people's belief that it is God's will to bless his people. There are three ways in which we recognize God's will for our lives. However, I believe it is God's will that we all live blessed lives spiritually and physically: "Beloved, I pray that in every way you may succeed and prosper and be in good health [physically], just as [I know] your soul prospers [spiritually]" (3 John 1:2 AMP). First, there is God's purposive will, which refers to God's desire and his decision for us to live blessed lives on purpose. Second, we have God's prescriptive will. That refers to God's desire and human decisions. Sometimes we make poor choices in life that block, hinder, and stop God's blessings from flowing into our lives. Finally, there's God's permissive will, which refers to human desire and God's permission. Sometimes our desires and choices in life are not God's purposeful will for us to live blessed lives. But God will allow certain things, choices, and actions of ours to be blessings to us. In such times, we are reminded that the all-knowing and all-seeing God can cause things to work out for us to live blessed lives.

> In the same way the Spirit [comes to us and] helps us in our weakness. We do not know what prayer to offer or how to offer it as we should, but the Spirit Himself [knows our need and at the right time] intercedes on our behalf with sighs and groanings too deep for words. And He who searches the hearts knows

what the mind of the Spirit is, because the Spirit intercedes [before God] on behalf of God's people in accordance with God's will. And we know [with great confidence] that God [who is deeply concerned about us] causes all things to work together [as a plan] for good for those who love God, to those who are called according to His plan and purpose. (Romans 8:26–28 AMP)

First Kingdom

Most of us, especially new believers who desire a closer walk with God the Father, ask "What is the kingdom of God, and where is it?" There are several things to consider when talking about the kingdom or the kingdom of God. These terms can refer to (1) the kingdom of heaven, where God the Father and Jesus live, sitting on the throne in the heavenly atmosphere, (2) a spiritual kingdom that resides in the very hearts and minds of God's people, or (3) the earthly kingdom in Israel during the Old Testament era, which wanted to be free from the rule of Roman governance though uprisings and political rebellion.

First there is the kingdom of God in heaven, where our heavenly Father sits on the throne and his Son, Jesus, sits beside him on the right-hand side. Mark 16:19 says that the kingdom of heaven is a real place where the saints go to be with God the Father once they leave the earthly realm. To be absent from the body is to be present with the Lord. Heaven is a place where no earthly presence, earthly tent, or our physical bodies can go or reside (Corinthians 5:3). Only spiritual bodies can reside in heaven. However, if we belong to God before we check out of here, die, pass from, or rest in peace, it is promised that we will be with him one day in heaven. The Word of God teaches us many truths, and we need to know, believe, and trust what God and his Word say regarding heaven.

A New Body

For we know that if the earthly tent [our physical body] which is our house is torn down [through death], we have a building from God, a house not made with hands, eternal in the heavens. For indeed in this house we groan, longing to be clothed with our [immortal, eternal] celestial dwelling, so that by putting it on we will not be found naked. For while we are in this tent, we groan, being burdened [often weighed down, oppressed], not that we want to be unclothed [separated by death from the body], but to be clothed, so that what is mortal [the body] will be swallowed up by life [after the resurrection]. Now He who has made us and prepared us for this very purpose is God, who gave us the [Holy] Spirit as a pledge [a guarantee, a down payment on the fulfillment of His promise].So then, being always filled with good courage and confident hope, and knowing that while we are at home in the body we are absent from the Lord—for we walk by faith, not by sight [living our lives in a manner consistent with our confident belief in God's promises]—we are [as I was saying] of good courage and confident hope, and prefer rather to be absent from the body and to be at home with the Lord. Therefore, whether we are at home [on earth] or away from home [and with Him], it is our [constant] ambition to be pleasing to Him. (2 Corinthians 5:1–9 AMP)

In John 14:2–3, Jesus tells us that in his Father's house, he has prepared a place for us. In this scripture, he is talking about a dwelling place in heaven. Through experiences, eyewitness accounts, and dreams of countless men and women, we have come to know that heaven is a real place we all hope to see one day. Some of the description gives the impression that heaven, with its streets of gold and pearly gates, is a place that will make the Taj Mahal look like a poor man's house. No words can really describe what heaven will look like. But again, with our limited wisdom, we have come to learn that heaven is an awesome place, a wonderful, beautiful place. In heaven there is no pain, no hate, no trouble, and no worries of this world order of things bad or negative. That may be hard for some to believe or even imagine.

God the Father is a Spirit that resides in heaven. As mentioned previously, we, however, are three-part beings. We are spiritual beings who possess souls and live in bodies (physical forms; 1 Thessalonians 5:23). Spirits can't live here on the earth because it would be illegal for them to do so. They were not created to live and operate in the earthly realm. Being that the earth is a physical place, all living beings need physical bodies to live in the earthly realm. This is how God the Father created the world in which we live. Just as a physical form or body can't live in the heavenly realm, spirits can't live and operate in the earthly realm without bodies. They would be out of order. It is illegal for a disembodied spirit to operate and live in the earthly realm without a body. Even when one dies, the spirit will go to heaven or hell, depending on the choice the person made before death.

> So, it is written [in Scripture], "The first man, Adam, became a living soul (an individual);" the last Adam (Christ) became a life-giving spirit [restoring the dead to life]. However, the spiritual [the immortal life] is not first, but the physical [the mortal life]; then the spiritual. The first man [Adam] is from the earth, earthy [made of dust]; the second Man [Christ, the Lord] is from heaven. As is the earthly man [the man of dust], so are those who are of earth; and as is the heavenly [Man], so are those who are of heaven. Just

as we have borne the image of the earthly [the man of dust], we will also bear the image of the heavenly [the Man of heaven]. Now I say this, believers, that flesh and blood cannot inherit *nor* be part of the kingdom of God; nor does the perishable (mortal) inherit the imperishable (immortal). (1 Corinthians 15:45–50 AMP)

We must realize that the choice of where we will go after death—heaven or hell—is ours. Once death has come, the physical form will go back to the dust of the earth from which it was created. So out of the earth, humanity was created in the image of God. Now the interesting thing here is man, a physical being, did not become a living being until God blew the breath of life into him. Genesis 1:26–27 says that "the Lord God formed man from the dust of the ground and breathed into his nostrils the breath of life and then man became a living being." In other words, man is a spiritual being who lives in a body and possesses a soul. Man is a three-part being because he was created in the image and likeness of God, who is a divine three-part entity. He is God the Father, God the Son, and God the Holy Spirit. Genesis 2:27 says, "Then God said let us make man in our image and in our likeness." Since we are three-part beings with spirits that possess souls and live in bodies (physical forms), each entity has needs, desires, and responsibilities.

Terms to Know

Pneuma (Greek term)—spirit known as the part of a person that relates to God; the invisible part of a person; spirit; Holy Spirit; the breath of God (Genesis 2:7; John 20:22).

Zoe (Greek term)—life of God; eternal life (John 5:24).

Adamah—man's earthly house; the first human body was formed out of the ground, the earth, and land (Genesis 2:7).

Pneumatiko—spiritual man; supernatural (Romans 8:16).

Psuche (Greek term)—the soul part of man, the natural realm of man, the flesh, physical form/physical being; the part of man that relates to his mind, his will, and his emotions.

Psuchikos (Greek term)—natural man, a soul man.

Clay (Hebrew term)—process in which man became a living soul, alive, or quicken in spirit Psalm 36:9; Genesis 2:7; Job 12:10).

Zoe Psuche (Greek term)—man is a three-part being—spirit, soul, and body (1 Corinthians 15:45–47; Hebrew 4:12; 1 Thessalonians 5:23).

The Second Kingdom

There is another kingdom in which we can live and operate while we are spiritual beings that live in bodies and possess souls. This kingdom is located in the heart and mind of someone who chooses to do so. It is not located in the heart of everyone, but it can be. The person who lives in this kingdom can only live there by choice; no one is forced to live there. Remember that this kingdom is located in the hearts of those who have decided to live there. Everyone who is capable of making the decision whether to live in or for the kingdom will have to choose God the Father and his kingdom. A life without God and his kingdom is really choosing hell, the kingdom of darkness.

I believe there is one basic truth we must realize: We are all God's creations, but by choice, we don't all belong to him. So, with that in mind, all of us are not children of God. To be a child of God is a decision only we can make. Unfortunately, some people have chosen not to belong to God the Father.

Let's face it, there are some who just do not acknowledge or love

God because they may have problems with their lives or with God. Lord, have mercy on them. There are choices everyone must make; and they include whether they want to live in God's kingdom or not. It is our free will that determines where we want to live. God blessed us all with the gift of choice and free will. The Word of God reassures us of this very truth in Luke 17:20–21 (NKJV): "And when he was demanded of the Pharisees, when the kingdom of God should come, he answered them and said, the kingdom of God cometh not with observation: Neither shall they say, Lo here! or, lo there! for, behold, 'the Kingdom of God is within you.'" This kingdom is in the hearts of every believer. That is why the Word says that the kingdom is not meat and drink but righteousness, peace, and joy in the Holy Spirit (Romans 14:17).

The Third Kingdom

The kingdom this book will be mostly exploring is the spiritual kingdom, the kingdom of God within you, and God's kingdom on earth, which his people obey and establish a new system of living. The Word of God tell us a lot about the earthly kingdom that we have neglected. We need to acknowledge, talk about, and take possession of the kingdom should be in the hearts and minds of every believer. As believers and saints of God, we would all love to go to heaven one day to be with God the Father. But I'm sure not all of us are ready or in a hurry to go there just yet. However, some of us have decided to live a blessed and experience the blessing of possessing the promises of the kingdom here on earth as God intended, with righteousness, joy, and peace in the Holy Ghost/Spirit (Daniel 6:26).

Throughout the Word, the Bible, the written voice of God, he has been telling us that we are entitled to blessings, wealth, and benefits, and we can possess a prosperous, blessed life now. But the world's understanding and standards of a blessed, prosperous life is different from God's. To the world, it is so much more than material possessions, as the Word of God reminds and informs us. And despite what some might think, we don't have to die to possess the blessings of God, the pie in the sky. It is well time to possess that which God the Father created for us to possess here in the earthly realm. Jesus tells us in John 10:10 that he came that we may have life, an abundant life, and to live life to the fullest. But we will never know this life unless we connect with the One who promised it to us.

In Mark 10:29–30, we are also promised love, joy, peace, land, and abundant prosperity in this life and in the life to come. When God's people believe and understand we were the original owners and possessors of the earth, until Adam and Eve fell from grace, there will be no problem in retaking possession of the promises of God (Genesis 1:26). We come to know in the third chapter of Genesis, dealing with the fall of humankind, that humans were dispossessed of the earthly realm. One very important fact we must also realize is that there are some things money can't buy and that power can have.

Money is not the kingdom of God. But remember, righteousness, peace, and joy in the Holy Ghost is where the kingdom truly is, and things, success, and prosperity will come. There is nothing wrong with having prosperity. But we should not let prosperity and things possess us. We must have a passion and desire to seek first God, his will, and his way of living: "But seek first his kingdom and his righteousness, and all these things will be given to you as well" (Matthew 6:33).

Becoming a Citizen of the Kingdom

There is only one way someone can become a citizen of God's kingdom, and that is by belonging to him. Accepting the gift of salvation and being born again through Jesus Christ is the only way in which one can become a citizen in God's kingdom. In John 14:4–6, Jesus clearly tells us that there is only one way to God the Father, and that is by accepting his Son Jesus Christ as Lord and Savior, which is the salvation process. John 1:12–13 (AMP) tells us:

But to as many as did receive and welcome Him, He gave the right [the authority, the privilege] to become children of God, that is, to those who believe in (adhere to, trust in, and rely on) His name—who were born, not of blood [natural conception], nor of the will of the flesh [physical impulse], nor of the will of man [that of a natural father], but of God [that is, a divine and supernatural birth—they are born of God—spiritually transformed, renewed, sanctified].

Unfortunately, some will never come to accept and know God the Father and become citizens of heaven. Philippians 3:17–20 reads,

Join one another in following my example, brothers, and carefully observe those who walk according to the pattern we set for you. For as I have often told you before, and now say again even with tears: Many live as enemies of the cross of Christ. Their end is destruction, their god is their belly, and their glory is in their shame. Their minds are set on earthly things. But our citizenship is in heaven, and we eagerly await a Savior from there, the Lord Jesus Christ, who, by the power that enables Him to subject all things to Himself, will transform our lowly bodies to be like His glorious body.

See the chapter "Prayers and Instruction for a Redeemed Life" in the back of the book.

"I'm the way and the truth and the life. No one come to the father except through me" (John 14:6). Here, Jesus is talking about coming into the kingdom through him. During biblical time, there were several religious sects. One of the early Christian sects that followed Jesus was called the Way. Jesus is still the only way to God the Father.

It is widely believed that as individuals become Christians, they must go through the salvation process of entering the kingdom of God through prayer and believing in their hearts, and by taking a conscious position of giving themselves totally over to God the Father. In this process, we automatically do two things. First, we renounce citizenship in the world's kingdom and ways of doing things and living. And second, we promise to accept a new lifestyle in God's kingdom. Once we come into the kingdom of God, we enter into a new covenant with him, and in this covenant, the Father promises to bless us, his children, children of promise. So in other words, we are now children of promise, children of God.

A covenant, in this context, is an agreement between God and us. In God's Word, he laid out the terms and guidelines of this agreement. Once we have entered into a covenant, a relationship with God as our Father, we have exchanged our ways of living and doing things for his. Yes, we still live in the world, but we are supposed to have a different standard of living once we have given ourselves over to God the Father. We must learn to live for the kingdom and train our minds and hearts for kingdom living. We answer to a much higher authority, while at the same time, we respect and obey the laws of the land. "Do not conform to the pattern of this world but be transformed by the renewing of your mind. Then you will be able to test and approve what God's will is—his good, pleasing, and perfect will" (Romans 12:2). This higher standard of living calls us not to conform to this world.

This mindset is when we first began to change. Or shall I say, we submit and surrender to God? If we acknowledge God in all our ways, the Word tells us that he will direct our paths. In the process of submitting to God, we allow his Word to transform us. The Word of God transforms us by being sown into our minds, which then is sown down into our hearts. "Thou word oh Lord have I hide in my heart that I might not sin against thee" (Psalm 119:11).

Some, however, have sown seeds of this world system in their minds and hearts while lying to themselves that they have surrendered all to Jesus. As humans, we surrender little of ourselves as we go, instead, holding back on God. But as we allow the mind of Christ to be in us, we can live for the kingdom of God out of pure hearts. When we feel as though the world has gotten the best of us, we can cry out like David did, asking God to "create in me a clean heart oh God and renew a right spirit within me" (Psalm 51:10).

However, in Ephesians 2:11–21, the act of totally of giving oneself over to God is really laid out for us and explained so beautifully. It also best explains how and why we have access to God the Father and his promises:

> Therefore, remember that you who are gentiles by birth and called "Uncircumcised" by those who call themselves "the Circumcision" (that is done in the body by hands of men)—remember that at that time you were separate from Christ, excluded from citizenship in Israel and foreigners to the covenant of the promise, without hope and without God in the world. But now in Christ Jesus you who once were far away have been brought near through the Blood of Christ Jesus. For he himself is our peace, who has made the two one and as destroyed the barrier, the dividing wall of hostility, by abolishing in his flesh the law with its commandments and regulations. His purpose was to create in himself one new man out of the two, thus making peace, and in this one body to reconcile both of them to God through the cross, by which he put to death their hostility. He came and preached peace to you who were far away peace to those who were near. For through him (Jesus) we both have access to the Father by one Spirit. Consequently, you are no longer

foreigners and aliens, but fellow citizens with God's people and members of God's household, built on the foundation of the apostles and prophets, with Christ Jesus himself as the Chief Cornerstone. In him the whole building is joined together and raised to become a Holy Temple in the Lord. And in him you too are being built together to become a dwelling in which God lives by his Spirit.

For the most part, through the covenant, it is God who wants us to know, understand, and realize that if he can live in us, dwell in us, bless and love others through us and our lives, we have fulfilled the covenant as he intended.

Responsibilities of the Kingdom

Father thy kingdom come; thou will be done on earth as it is in Heaven. (Matthew 6:1)

As children of God and citizens of his kingdom, we have responsibilities to God our Father and to his kingdom in the earthly realm. We should never want to belong or be a part of something of which we do not take an active role or participate in its development and care. It is our responsibility to pray, promote, and support the kingdoms of God. It is also vital to remember that there is more than one kingdom to promote and support in our hearts and minds, the one here on earth and the other in heaven. And even though we are here on earth, we can help both kingdoms. We promote the kingdom of heaven by sharing our faith and informing others of the afterlife, life eternal. We care for and support the kingdom of God in the earthly realm by living as godly citizens, honoring God and supporting the laws of the land. Of course, we study God's Word, worshipping and honoring him in our daily lives as we build heaven in our hearts and minds. Even though we all would love to go to heaven one day, most of us are not in a hurry to go there just yet. So for now, we want to live here and experience the blessings of possessing the promises of the covenant and kingdom here on earth.

Many saints do not realize that we are going to be held accountable for whether we prayed, promoted, and supported the kingdom here on earth. One day we all will give an account of how we lived in the earthly realm. Second Corinthians 5:10 (AMP) tells us, "For we [believers will be called to account and] must all appear before the judgment seat of Christ, so that each one may be repaid for what has been done in the body, whether good or bad [that is, each will be held responsible for his actions, purposes, goals, motives—the use or misuse of his time, opportunities and abilities]."

There are several ways that we can promote and support God's kingdom while we're here on earth. They include prayer, obedience, faithfulness, righteousness, and love.

Prayer is the number-one way we can promote and support the kingdom of God because prayer can do so many things. In all reality, covenant people and people of prayer should try not to do anything without first praying. Prayer can bring change to both the earthly and spiritual realms in any situation and circumstance. Prayer can bring growth, healing, and even evoke the very presence and power of God in any and every circumstance. When we pray for the kingdom, we agree with God's plan and will for his kingdom and that his will be done on earth. "The prayer of a righteous man is powerful and effective"; it brings change. In James 5:16–17, the Word reminds us of Elijah, a man just like us who prayed, and his prayers affected the natural law, the earthly realm. Our prayers not only affect the spiritual realm but the earthly, natural realm as well and in many visible ways.

We should operate in and live a life that will glorify God. Live a life that will exemplify the kingdom. Titus 3:1–7 tells us, "Be subject to rulers and authorities, to be obedient, to be ready to do whatever is good, to slander no one, to be peaceable and considerate and to show true humility toward all men." Stop putting Christ on public disgrace by living any kind of way we want. When we do, we subject him to a public crucifixion all over again (Hebrews 6:6). How are you representing the kingdom in your daily life? We must continuously ask ourselves, "Would someone want to become a citizen of the kingdom of God by watching how I live?" We are a representation and a reflection of God's kingdom. It has been said that God's character set the standard for what is right and just. As Christians, our characters should also set the standard for those around us. Remember how your earthly parents would tell you not to act like a fool when out in public? Well, it is my belief that God the Father has also told us about the same thing in the Word: "It is impossible for those who have once been enlightened, who have tasted the heavenly gift, who have shared in the Holy Spirit, who have tasted the goodness of the word of God and the powers of the coming age and who have fallen away, to be brought back to repentance. To their loss they are crucifying the Son of God all over again and subjecting him to public disgrace" (Hebrews 6:4–6). We must be conscious and aware of our representations of Jesus and the kingdom of God. Just as Christ Jesus was the Word that became flesh and lived among people, we also ought to become the Word, a living epistle ready to be read by all men (John 1:1; 2 Corinthians 3:2). God said that he is holy although he lived among and in his covenant people. Immanuel, God with us. And although he dwells in his people, he's totally opposite from his people. He reminds his covenant people that he is not human but holy, and as covenant people, we become holy because God is holy. We don't make God who he is; he makes us who we are, "holy covenant people."

> God is not human, that he should lie, not a human being, that he should change his mind. Does he speak and then not act? Does he promise and not fulfill?" (Numbers 23:19)

"For my thoughts are not your thoughts, neither are your ways my ways," declares the Lord. "As the heavens are higher than the earth, so are my ways higher than your ways and my thoughts than your thoughts." (Isaiah 55:8–9 ASV)

Use your resources—such as your time, money, gifts, talents, and skills—so that God's earthly kingdom can function properly. The kingdom of heaven is already covered. And God the Father has blessed his people with so much so that they can help establish his kingdom here on earth. That brings him glory. It takes your resources to bless the kingdom of God. Look at the United States, for instance, its people's wealth and resources. America is known as one of the wealthiest countries in the world. The average poor family in the United States lives far better than the standard of living of a person in a third world country. People who have seen poverty in different places in the world will tell you that to live in the United States is a blessing. Not only is it a great place to live because of its resources, we have the privilege of freedom many places in the world don't have. In America, we can live different lifestyles and participate in practices that we could be killed for if we lived anywhere else. It is our responsibility to bring God's kingdom here on earth. Are you doing your part?

A Major Promise of the Kingdom: Baptism of the Holy Spirit

After his suffering he showed himself to these men and gave many convincing proofs that he was alive. He appeared to them over a period of forty days and spoke about the Kingdom of God. On one occasion, while he was eating with them, he gave them this command: Do not leave Jerusalem, but wait for the gift my father promised, which you have heard me speak about. For John baptized with water, but in a few days, you will be baptized with the Holy Spirit. (Acts 1:3–8)

We operate and fully live in the kingdom of God on earth after we have been baptized in the Holy Spirit. The Holy Spirit gives us the power to live and operate under kingdom principles. Being baptized in the Spirit of God the Father and filled with his Spirit are two ways of knowing God. All believers have the infilling of the Holy Spirit once they have come to the knowledge and acceptance of our Lord and Savior, Jesus Christ. However, all Christians and those who have accepted Jesus in their hearts have not been baptized in the Spirit. To be baptized in the Spirit is to experience another level of intimacy with God. It is a whole other level of surrendering one's life completely to God the Father. Some know him as Savior, but there are still some believers who need to know him as Lord, our Father. To know Jesus as Lord is to surrender one's life completely to the Father, without holding anything back. This step requires total trust in God.

There is nothing to fear in surrendering one's life over to God because fear has torment. God loves us, so we have nothing to fear. God actual reminds us that he did not even give us a spirit of fear (2 Timothy 2:7), but he did give us a spirit of power, love, and a sound mind. God has come into our lives to bless us, not to torment us (1 John 4:18). The enemy, however, desires and torment us with whatever he can. Again, John 10:10 reminds of that the thief—the enemy— only comes into our lives to steal, kill, and destroy our lives. Jesus, however, told us he came so we might have and enjoy life and to live life in abundance, to the full, until it overflows. There is nothing to fear in surrendering one's life to God because he does not come into our lives to torment us but to love and bless us. The enemy only comes to torment and destroy our lives (John 10:10; 1 John 4:18).

The infilling of the Holy Spirit and the baptism of the Spirit are somewhat different. You can have something, but possessing that very thing will make a big difference. Now I just don't have the Holy Spirit, the Holy Spirit has me, but only with my permission. Does God the Father have your full, complete permission to have your life? To have love and to operate in love is two different things. For example, I love beurre Bosc, or Bosc pears. I *really* love them. They taste good to me; they look like they taste good to me. But until I consumed one, took possession of and ate one, I would have never experienced or known the fullness of having a Bosc pear to enjoy. To possess or consume a thing is different than just having it or knowing and being aware of it. After one has experienced something to the level of consuming it, that thing has now become part of the life experience. Now that it has taken part of you, intimacy has developed.

Learning and getting to know the Spirit of God the Father in an intimate way is such a blessing. Despite experiencing pain and suffering in your life, a sense of peace can now reside in you. Surrounding circumstances that are haunting and designed to destroy you, must now back away from you because you now realize they cannot hurt you as you thought. You now understand and realize that the peace of God has come into your life simply to bless and guide you. You have decided to cast all your cares on to God because he truly and really does care for his people (1 Peter 5:7). This new level of knowing God brings comfort and direction amid confusion, hope amid devastation, and peace during a storm.

CHAPTER 2

Terms of the Covenant: A Covenant Connection

Numbers 23:19
Deuteronomy 5:1–3; 10:12–14; 29:9; 30:11–14
Psalm 111:4–9
Isaiah 1:19
John 1:13
Romans 14:7–9
1 Corinthians 3:1–3
2 Corinthians 4:4
Ephesians 4:11–16, 24–25
Hebrews 8:10; 9:15
Colossians 1:21–22
1 Peter 2:2
3 John 1:2

He has caused his wonders to be remembered; the Lord is gracious and compassionate. He provides food (provision) for those who fear him (worship him); he remembers his covenant forever. He has shown his people the power of his works, giving them the lands (heritage) of other nations. (Psalm 111:4–9 AMP; Psalm 111:4–6)

If you are willing and obedient, you will eat the good things of the land; but if you resist and rebel, you will be devoured by the sword. For the mouth of the Lord has spoken. (Isaiah 1:19)

This is the covenant I will establish with the people of Israel after that time, declares the Lord. I will put my laws in their minds and write them on their hearts. I will be their God, and they will be my people. (Hebrews 8:10)

When reading the Word of God, we must ask ourselves these simple questions. First, "Am I a child of the covenant?" If the answer is yes, ask yourself, "Am I living a life below what God has intended for me, and am I glorifying God the Father in my daily life?" If the answer to this question is yes, ask yourself, "Why don't I possess the promises of the kingdom under the terms of the covenant?" What covenant? The covenant of salvation that exists in the Word of God. The term "covenant" is a Latin term meaning coming together. Two or more parties coming together in a contract, an agreement with responsibilities and privileges.

It is not hard for us to realize that it is to our benefit to come into agreement with the Most High God because he has a lot more to offer us than we do him. We need God more than he needs us. God needs us to help fulfill and bring his kingdom here on earth through prayer, good works, and living a holy lifestyle. Because he is a Spirit, he would not violate his own law of operating in the earthly realm without a physical form. We need God to live a victorious and an abundant life in the earthly realm. As covenant people, we have entered a covenant with God through the gift of salvation, and the terms of this covenant entitle us to certain benefits and privileges on earth. God is obligated to bless us since we are children of the covenant (Psalm 111:4–6). Just as we are obligated to live within the terms of the covenant, God is obligated to bless us. God's will for his people is not so far out there that it is unobtainable. It is basic and such a simple understanding that even a child can learn and understand it. Let us be clear: A blessed life, I believe, is a life that is enjoyable. Possessing a blessed life is not materialistic or just about having material things. It is about having a wealthy soul because you have righteousness, love, joy, and peace in the Holy Ghost.

God has not left his people in doubt and uncertainty about his will for their lives. Deuteronomy chapters 29 and 30 are very insightful about what it means to be in a covenant with God the Father. Chapter 29, verse 9 tells us, "Carefully follow the terms of this covenant, so that you may prosper in everything you do." And Deuteronomy 30:11–14 state,

> For this commandment which I command you today
> is not too difficult for you, nor is it out of reach. It
> is not in heaven, that you should say, "Who will go
> up to heaven for us to get it for us and make us hear
> it, that we may observe it?" Nor is it beyond the sea,
> that you should say, "Who will cross the sea for us to
> get it for us and make us hear it, that we may observe
> it." But the word is very near you, in your mouth and
> in your heart, that you may observe it.

The Bible tells us in Hebrews 10:16 that God himself took time to write the laws of the covenant on our minds and put them in our hearts. This says to me that the Bible is alive, living inside us, which in turn makes the new covenant alive as it lives inside us. This belief is also supported in 1 Corinthians 3:2–3, which says that we should become living epistles, ready to be read by all people. Jesus was the Word that became flesh and lived among his people (John 1:13). But too often we, as covenant people, want the benefits, blessings, wealth, and all God's promises without taking responsibilities that come with the terms of our covenant agreements with God. One's covenant with God was activated the moment you received Jesus Christ as your personal Lord and Savior. Hebrews 9:15 says, "For this reason Christ is the mediator of a new covenant, that those who are called may receive the promised eternal inheritance, now that he has died as a ransom to set them free from the sins committed under the first covenant."

When people come to the altar and say they want Jesus as their Lord and Savior, they often are hesitant to make him Lord over all their lives' matters, not just by what they're saying at that moment, while everyone is looking at them. It is by how people live their lives after they walk away from the altar. For those seeking to live blessed lives, they would have to surrender their all and all to God—their whole lives and everything concerning them. Then we will have rights and privileges of the kingdom of God through his covenant. Of course we experience some levels of blessing after entering a new relationship with God, but not like what we would experience were we to surrender our all to God. Romans 10:9–13 reminds us:

> If you confess with your mouth Jesus *as* Lord and believe in your heart that God raised Him from the dead, you will be saved; for with the heart a person believes, resulting in righteousness, and with the mouth he confesses, resulting in salvation. For the Scripture says, "Whoever believes in him will not be disappointed." For there is no distinction between Jew and Greek; for the same Lord is Lord of all, abounding in riches for all who call on Him; for "Whoever will call on the name of the Lord will be saved."

I believe that for many of us, at the time of receiving salvation, we confessed Jesus as Lord of our lives. But it is in time that we learn to know if we really have given him our hearts and minds. Time will tell if we truly trust God. It is the goodness of our Lord that draws us to repentance and wanting to give him our hearts and minds. We can or will not be able to give God our hearts without first giving him our minds. Later, we will learn that our hearts and minds are two in one in that they are one with two functions.

> Then Moses summoned all Israel and said to them: "Hear, O Israel, the statutes and judgments (legal decisions) which I am speaking today in your hearing, so that you may learn them and observe them carefully. The Lord our God made a covenant with us at Horeb. The Lord did not make this covenant with our fathers, but with us, all of us who are alive here today." (Deuteronomy 5:1–3)

> And now, Israel, what does the Lord your God require from you, but to fear [and worship] the Lord your God [with awe-filled reverence and profound respect], to walk [that is, to live each, and every day] in all His ways and to love Him, and to serve the Lord your God with all your heart and with all your soul [your choices, your thoughts, your whole being] and to keep the commandments of the Lord and His statutes which I am commanding you today for your good? Behold, the heavens and the highest of heavens belong to the Lord your God, the earth and all that is in it. (Deuteronomy 10:12–14 AMP)

In a covenant, there are benefits and obligation, terms and conditions that are legal and binding. As defined previously, to enter a covenant with someone is to enter in to an agreement. Under a covenant agreement, if either party does not fulfill any part of the agreement, then legally, the persons involved can call on their covenant rights of canceling their covenant agreement. However, the covenant we have entered in to with God is eternally binding (Psalm 111:9).

The Word of God also tells us that while we were yet sinners and in our weakest states of being, Christ died to give us eternal lives and the gift of salvation; he created a covenant. God the Father will never cancel our covenant with him. He already knows we are weak but loves us anyway and forever. Once you entered into a covenant agreement with God, you turned your lives over to him. There is no turning back, not that anyone would want to unless that person has lost his or her mind. But should someone decide to do so, that individual would later realize the loss of the blessings and goodness of God. But hallelujah and thanks be to God for repentance and forgiveness.

Unfortunately, a lot of people have been tricked and fooled into turning back to their former ways of life, lives of sin and destruction. But after a moment of delusion, they soon desperately want to be delivered from what they have become entangled in again by turning back to destruction. When we return to our former lives, we turn our backs on the covenant and refuse to follow the terms of the agreement we made with God. And we know he will never turn his back on anyone. Thank God for his forgiveness, grace, and mercy that we can come back to him for anything and everything. "For God is not a man that he should lie or the son of man that he should change his mind or repent" (Numbers 23:19).

In Romans 14:7–9, we come to understand what and who we have joined ourselves to—a family of believers. None of us live to ourselves or die to ourselves because if we live or die to ourselves, we have not truly confessed Jesus Christ as Lord of our lives. Christ died and arose for us so that we may have eternal life, join the family of God, and become citizens of the kingdom. At one time we were alienated from God; and considered his enemies. But because he gave his life so that we may have eternal life with the Father, we have been reconciled to God through him, "Christ Jesus" (Colossians 1:21–23).

However and whatever we choose to do, entering in to a covenant agreement with God Almighty, our heavenly Father, is very serious business. The gift of salvation is really not a joking matter. It is not something you do just to be doing it or do it half-heartedly. It's not a playing matter because we are talking about our lives, the one here and now and the one to come, which is eternal life. I'm convinced there are some Christians who have been in a relationship with God after their actions, or should I say, after their leaps of faith. That is why it's every believer's responsibility to seek God through prayer, Bible study, and regular attendance of a Christian, Bible-believing church. Fellowshipping with some strong brothers and sisters in the Lord is good because we are one body or one big family. Hebrews 10:25 reminds us not to forsake the assembly of ourselves together so that we can grow spiritually and fellowship with each other just like a regular family. We should know and learn the importance of connecting, loving, and communicating with each other as a family. No one should ever feel alone with no support, love, and care.

God has said that he has given us pastors after his own heart to mature us and to help us grow spiritually (Jeremiah 3:15). Beloved, it's not our Father's will that we remain infants. Once we are born again in the spiritual realm, we must give an account as to how we handle our spiritual growth after the gift of salvation. You and I can no longer waver in our faith, being lured away from God and operating in our old natures, the corrupted selves that are carnally minded. For the Word of God says, we did not come to know God the Father this way.

Now, because of the revelation of the Word of God, many Christians are going around making positive confessions and affirmation, calling on their covenant privileges. But at the same time, they have neglected to align with the Word of God in their daily lives;

they are living like nothing. Old saints used to say when we neglected to align with the Word of God, "You aren't living nothing, child." In other words, if we are going to confess the Word and watch it manifest from what you are believing, we need to have corresponding actions to follow our confessions of faith. Our confession of faith is saying the same thing as God is saying in his Word. If we are saying the same as God says, it should be no problem in living how he wants us to live. No more lip service.

The book of James put it this way: Faith without works is dead. Some of God's people are living every kind of way, without holiness and not practicing the righteousness in which we all were made through Christ. Some come to God with no substance; their hearts are far from God (Isaiah 29:13). When we accepted Jesus Christ as Savior, we exchanged who we were for who he is, the righteousness of God. Some of our brothers and sisters are living dangerous lives while saying things like, "I'm a child of the Most High God," "I'm the head and not the tail," "I walk in wealth," and, "I'm blessed going in, and I'm blessed coming out." All these statements of faith are true because it is the Word of God, and we should make these statements until they manifest in our lives. But don't just give God lip service. Live what you are confessing. God the Father will not be made a fool of.

If I can be truthful for a moment, some are really living in a delusion and have decided in their own minds to play games with our heavenly Father and themselves. Our Father said he will not be mocked; whatever you sow you will reap, and that's real. Now don't get me wrong. We are to make positive affirmations and agree with God's Word and his plans for our lives. But how can we expect the promises and blessings of God if we are not living in line with his covenant and its promises and terms? We are to be kingdom people living with a new covenant as a holy people, a royal nation, like God the Father.

Exodus 19:5 (NLT) tells us, "now if you obey me fully and keep my covenant, then out of all nations you will be my treasured possession.

Although the whole earth is mine, you will be for me a Kingdom of priests and a Holy Nation." Hallelujah! It should make you smile and feel special inside to be called God's, "treasured possession." To be known that way should make anyone feel a lot better, especially after being beat down by daily life. I don't know about you, but I feel good and elated knowing that one fact and promise from our heavenly Father. In one way or another, most of us have experienced some form of rejection and oppression. And a word from God's heart as being a treasured possession is very encouraging. That makes one walk around with his or her head held high and chest stuck out. After all, you are loved by someone as awesome as God the Father, who created the heavens and earth. Amen.

However, believe it or not, there are some who feel as if they are not living a blessed life, and God the Father is blamed. He is blamed for not keeping his end of the covenant. Though we know is not true, he is blamed most of the time. Most of us play the blame game, and when things don't go our way or the way we hoped them to, it is always someone else's fault. God has said that he honors his word above his name. Numbers 23:19 says that God is not a man that he should lie, nor the Son of man that he should change his mind or repent. He has spoken, and it came to pass. God is faithful. He has not and will never break the terms of his covenant with us.

If the promises of the covenant have not shown up on your doorstep, it's not his fault. It is possibly demonic forces trying to withstand the post-salvation you. Or perhaps you are unaware that you are working against yourself. Psalm 89:30–34 tells us, "If my sons forsake my law and do not follow my statutes, if they violate my decrees and fail to keep my commands, I will punish their sin with the rod, their iniquity with flogging/punishment; whip, scourge but I will not take my love from him, nor will I ever betray my faithfulness. I will not violate my covenant or alter what my lips have uttered." So stop wasting time, blaming God for your shortcomings, faults, and weaknesses. Start taking responsibility for your own spiritual development and failures in life, your actions and reactions. Start living a blessed life today, an abundant life, the life that God intended for you to live.

John 10:10 tells us that Jesus said he came so we should live life and live it more abundantly. But the enemy—the devil—came to kill, steal, and destroy your life, your dreams, and your plans. And believe it or not, most of us have helped him big time to do just that. But no more because God has said that he knows the plans he has for us—good not evil, to prosper us, and to give us hope, an expected end (Jeremiah 29:11). The Word tells us in Ephesians 4:28 (NKJV), "Let him who stole steal no longer, but rather let him labor, working with his hands what is good, that he may have something to give him who has need."

A Covenant Connection: Living in Your Rightful Place

> Now if you obey me fully and keep my covenant; then out of all nations you will be my treasured possession, although the whole earth is mine. (Exodus 19:5)

> If you are willing and obedient, you will eat the good of the land; but if you refuse and rebel you will be devoured by the sword. For the mouth of the Lord has spoken. (Isaiah 1:19–20)

I love these scriptural passages because they really identify how much we mean to God the Father. There are several problems I believe that most folk have with God, and they are pinpointed in Exodus 19:5. Some have not come to grips with who God is, and some do not know who they are in him. And finally, some folks don't know how much they really mean to him. I have come to understand that most people do not believe or think God truly loves or cares for them as much as he does. For God to tell us that we are his treasured possessions on the earth—even though the whole earth is his—now that is awesome.

Every time I read that passage, I remember how special I am to God. We, as covenant people, have not fully come to understand who and whose we are in him. It is our heavenly Father's desire that we come to know who he really is. Not only does he want us to know him, he wants us to know who we are in him and what we have as his dearest children. Think about your children. What if your child knew nothing about you as a person, your family history and background, or understood or know about their privileges, benefits, and rights of being your child. If that were the case, you, as a parent, would probably be greatly offended and hurt.

Well, believe it or not, that is just how our heavenly Father feels regarding us not knowing who we are as his children and very little about him as a parent. Many privileges are promised to us for being God's children. But the enemy of this world has blinded the minds and hearts of people by speaking lies and distorting the truth of God and his Holy Word (2 Corinthians 3:14). Therefore, knowing the Word of God is important for our spiritual growth and development. Not only will we grow and develop spiritually by knowing his Word, we will also come to know our heavenly Father and who and why we are here on this earth and our purposes in this life. You will know the truth, and the truth will set you free. Free to know who you were created to be. When you do not know who you are, where you came from, and why you are here, you will always live beneath your rights and privileges. Persons living beneath who they were created to be are often lost, unhappy, and unproductive. Unfortunately, this type of person will just go through life existing. This ought not be. Living a life without knowing who you are is no way to live a blessed life.

God desires his children to know him and who they are in him. When people don't know who they are, they will live any kind of way, often with evil behaviors like pride and arrogance. But knowing who you are and living in God produces godly wisdom. That is true wealth.

It will cause one to possess a humble heart that leads to eternal wealth, which money cannot buy. God the Father really has an abundant life for us to live; he tells us this many times. Proverbs 8:17–21 reinforces this truth: "I love those who love me, and those who seek me find me. With me are riches and honor, enduring wealth, and prosperity. My fruit is better than fine gold; what I yield surpasses choice silver. I walk in the way of righteousness, along the paths of justice, bestowing a rich inheritance on those who love me and making their treasuries full." One of the most important things Proverbs 8:17–21 should remind us of is that wealth is not just about having a lot of money and material things. True wealth is also knowing, loving, and being grateful to God the Father for the lives he has given us. Or shall I say gifted us with. Also being aligned with God and having a good relationship with him, having a prosperous spirit and life, and enjoying the life he has blessed us with. Third John 1:2 describes a perfect example: "beloved I pray that you may prosper in every way and (that your body) may keep well, even as (I know) your soul keeps well and prospers" (AMP).

CHAPTER 3

Taking a Closer Look

Deuteronomy 30
Mark 10:29–31
John 1:14; 15:5
James 1:22–25
2 Corinthians 3:2–3

There have been three areas in which the enemy, Satan, the devil himself, has robbed and stolen our abundant lives from us. It has worked for centuries, ever since the beginning of time. Even though the enemy has done so, he is still limited in his power to harm and destroy us. But believe it or not, we empower him to harm, kill, steal, and destroy our lives. First, we give the enemy power in our lives through our minds, by what we conceive and create in our minds, in what we think about and allow to stay on our minds. Second, in our hearts by what we perceive, understand, and by what we harbor and allow to stay there in our hearts. Third and finally, we give the enemy power through our mouths by what we say and confess out of it, over and over, consciously and unconsciously agreeing with what comes out of our mouths and the mouths of others. What comes out of our mouths is very important because it affects our lives as it really exposes what is in our hearts.

Words are alive. They have creative powers; they are spirits. But we will get into all that later. If we realize the devil can do so much to us as children of God, we will walk in victory a lot more than we do. But whatever the devil is doing, he tries to do it well. If we practice self-control and discipline ourselves to walk in the authority that God has given us in these three areas—the mind, the heart, and the mouth—we will live a victorious life, a better life, an abundant life, a life God has intended for us.

In John 15:5, we see that for one to live an effective Christian life, we must learn that without Jesus Christ, we can do nothing. There are also several basic questions we should often ask ourselves because they will affect the quality of our lives. But most important, they will affect our spiritual lives. Remember, it is God's desire that even our souls will prosper.

Here are the questions:

> What is on your mind? What do you constantly think about and/or meditate on?
> What are you harboring in your heart? How do you feel about your God, others, and yourself? What are your true feelings and intentions concerning your faith and the issues of your life?
> What are you really saying when you speak? What are you talking about, and how do you say it? Who and what are you agreeing with?

If we were to master these three areas—the mind, the heart, and the mouth—by making a conscious decision of taking control and bringing them under the authority of the Holy Spirit and the obedience of Christ, I believe we will see a change for the better in our lives. These three areas affect both the natural and spiritual realms of life. And after the gift of salvation, it is our responsibility to become mature believers as we grow in these three areas that are vital to spiritual growth and development. It is my belief that we can develop and grow spiritually as mature Christians in these three areas. First, by making a conscious decision to make Christ our Savior; second, by prayer and seeking the help of God; and third, we will mature spiritually by reading, studying, and meditating on the Word of God through confessing and pondering over it. One will become a mature Christian after practicing all he or she has learned through prayer, seeking, meditating, and reading and studying the Word of God. The book of James reminds us that when a person acknowledges God's Word above individual opinion, and not just listen to the Word, he or she will be blessed and receive God's favor. In turn, one will experience a good life as God the Father desires and designed it to be.

> Do not merely listen to the word, and so deceive yourselves. Do what it says. Anyone who listens to the word but does not do what it says is like someone who looks at his face in a mirror and, after looking at himself, goes away and immediately forgets what he looks like. But whoever looks intently into the perfect law that gives freedom and continues in it— not forgetting what they have heard but doing it— they will be blessed in what they do. (James 1:22–25)

Our faith should be alive, not just something we read and talk about. James 1:22 says that we should not just be mere listeners of God's Word but doers as well. And by doing what God's Word says, we will be blessed.

In James chapter 2, we are also reminded that faith without works is dead. The body of Christ (Christian) is not dead because the God we serve is not dead. Christ Jesus is alive, and he wants to become alive in every believer.

The Bible tells us that Jesus was the Word that became flesh and dwelled among us (John 1:14). However, 2 Corinthians 3:2–3 tells us what most of us fail to realize: We can become the Word, just as Jesus was the Word that lived and dwelled among us in the earth. "You yourselves are our letter, written on our hearts, known and read by everyone. You show that you are a letter from Christ, the result of our ministry, written not with ink but with the Spirit of the living God, not on tablets of stone but on tablets of human hearts" (2 Corinthians 3:2–3).

Too many believers have the understanding that we go to church on Sunday and go through our religious routines and motions. Then, from the benediction of the Sunday service to Monday, straight to Saturday night, we live unto ourselves however we want. This should not be. As covenant people, we are responsible to God for how we live 24/7. If we are truly his people, called by his name, we don't live unto ourselves but unto God. Many of us want a relationship with God and a faith that's convenient, a faith with no responsibilities or accountability, which we can pick up when we want to and put back on the shelf when we are done. The Father, however, seeks those who are willing to serve and exchange their lives for his. Our heavenly Father is looking for someone who is committed to serve him in spirit and in truth, every hour of every day, and who is always available to him, no matter the time, no matter the sacrifice. Just like someone teaches their lover how to love him or her, God will show you how to love and serve him. God the Father loves us that much. He is the lover of our souls.

One of my professors made a profound statement one evening that has stuck with me. She said, "A person chooses to be chosen." After she said that, I realize how powerful it was. In other words, everyone wants to be favored and have the favor of God the Father on and in their lives, but most people aren't willing to go the extra mile to get to know and learn who God is. Throughout history, we have heard and seen many men and women of God experience the favor and blessing of God. From the time of Cain versus Abel, Noah, Moses, Queen Esther, and Daniel, an excellent servant of God who had integrity. Who can forget Paul, who dedicated himself to write most of the New Testament amid major persecution and rejection? But still, certain folk will sit back and wonder why them, why him or her and not them? I contend that it happened for them because they chose for it to happen for them. They chose to believe God and agree with his covenant for their lives. It is my belief that we have the choice to be blessed.

One important thing to realize is that we all are blessed because God has caused us to be among the land of the living. We are blessed with his love, his favor, and his grace in which they all are one in the same as the sun shines on us all. To have life is a blessing. In Ecclesiastes 9:4, the Word tells us that "Anyone who is among the living has hope—even a live dog is better off than a dead lion!"

One does not have to work for the blessings of the Lord. God is so gracious toward us that he has blessed us already. However, I believe some blessings are conditional. The Lord is a merciful and giving God. And because God is so giving, we can't outgive him. God places no limits to his giving, but *we* put limits on his giving through the way we believe and receive, how we accept and operate in the truth of God. Learning God's Word and getting wisdom from it helps us to live better lives. As a result of studying God's Word, we develop qualities that guide us to live good lives. From his mouth come knowledge and understanding, and as we continue to study God's Word, we learn that all successes and blessings are not just material. Most important, they are spiritual as well.

For the Lord gives wisdom from his mouth come knowledge and understanding. He holds success in store for the upright; he is a shield to those whose walk is blameless, for he guards the course of the just and protects the way of his faithful one. (Proverbs 2:6–8)

I believe when we hunger and thirst after God and his Word, we develop behaviors, mindsets, attitudes, and disciplined lifestyles to live blessed and prosperous lives. God's Word, with its wisdom, can even protect and deliver one from the wickedness of humanity. "Wisdom will save you from the ways of wicked men, from men whose words are perverse, who have left the straight paths to walk in dark ways, who delight in doing wrong and rejoice in the perverseness of evil, whose paths are crooked and who are devious in their ways" (Proverbs 2:12–15).

If we study the Word, we will see other promises of the covenant, for example, like in Mark 10:29–31. I believe this is a conditional blessing, as Jesus tells Peter, "no one who has left home or brothers or sisters or mother or father or children or fields for me and the gospel will fail to receive a hundred times as much in this present age homes, brothers, sisters, mothers, children and fields— and with them, persecutions and in the age to come, eternal life." Conditional blessings require us to act or react in a certain way. Like when the Word reminds us to give, and it will be given back to us. This reminds me of an old hymn we sang in church. The title of the song was "You Can't Beat God Giving," written by Doris Akers in 1957. A classic gospel song, it went something like this: "You can't beat God giving no matter how hard you try. The more you give God gives to you." The older I get, I have found this to be so true.

In Deuteronomy chapter 30, we also see that some blessings are conditional, for example, where God says he laid before us an open door, life, or death, blessing, or curses. That same scripture tells what to choose: Choose life. But there are still some people who will not take God's advice and choose life, thereby receiving a life beyond their wildest dreams. Some people are not aware, understand, or possibly know they have a choice to live a blessed life on purpose. This is so unfortunate and a disadvantage for some who do not know they have a choice to be purposely blessed.

CHAPTER 4

A Perfect Example

Exodus 34:14–16
Numbers 22:5–6, 12; 23:18–20, 25
Psalm 24:1
Matthew 5:28
John 10:10
1 Corinthians 6:18; 10:8; 15:33
Ephesians 4:18–22
Revelation 2:13–14, 20–21

Let's not make the same mistake as our forefathers.

In Numbers chapters 22 through 25, there is a perfect example as to how the enemy has robbed God's people for centuries. It tells the story of the Israelites and how they destroyed themselves. Somehow, this story still speaks to us and how we, too, can kill, steal, and help destroy our lives, dreams, hopes, and God's plans for us. The enemy does not have to do much of anything to help some of us destroy our lives. He knows that if we don't operate in and obey God's precepts, we will destroy ourselves. The enemy knows when we don't study, learn, and know God's Word, his truth. And if we don't know God's Word, the enemy will tell us lies; he will lie to us about everything. He lies to us about things from our health, to even our faith in the promises of God. When one doesn't submit and or surrender to God the Father, we open ourselves to some of the same old stuff that has been destroying people's lives since the begging of time. Things like rebellion, weakness of the flesh, disobedience, pride, stubbornness, and willful ignorance have destroyed and will continue to destroy people's lives. We want to live life in such a way that even our children will be blessed, thereby passing on generational blessings, not cures and destruction.

Look with me, if you will, in the Old Testament. We see the children of Israel doing very well before they crossed over into the land of Jordan. King Balak, son of Zippor, was over Moab and envied Israel. Not only did he envy them, he also dreaded them because of their great prosperity in the land of Moab. The Promised Land was not very far from Moab. Filled with fear, jealousy, and hatred for God's people, the Israelites, King Balak summoned a wicked prophet name, Balaam. He was known for sorcery and putting curses on people. Even though Balaam was well known for so-called black magic and things of that sort, he was also known for the respect he had for God's power and for God's people, the Israelites. So the false prophet Balaam was known to mix some truth with falsehoods from other religions.

King Balak sent the false prophet a message in Numbers 22:5–6, saying that "a people have come out of Egypt, they cover the face of the land and have settled next to me. Now come and put a curse on these people because they are too powerful for me. Perhaps then I will be able to defeat them and drive them out of the land."

Balak replied, "For I know that whoever you bless is blessed and whoever you curse is cursed." You see, child of God, the enemy is afraid of who you are as his prosperous child. Prosperity has authority when we walk in it. In the prosperous life, you must know who you are as a child of God and walk in the prosperous authority that God has given you. As we walk in this prosperous authority, we demonstrate who we are and to whom we belong, God the Father. Therefore, the enemy fights us very hard, certainly about possessing a prosperous life. Please remember possessing a prosperous life is not just about having things or things having us. First and foremost, we are prosperous because we have righteousness, joy, and peace in the Holy Ghost.

You must know who you are as a child of God and walk in the prosperous authority as God dear child. Take for instance, a two-year-old, and watch how they play and interact with others when they know that they are taken care of and loved by their parents. The child will play with such freedom, confidence, and reassurance of who he or she is. Such children move with such liberty and confidence. And they are very happy children. Well, my friend, that is how our heavenly Father wants us to live and enjoy our lives here, now on earth. Jesus said, "I come that they may have life and have it more abundantly (John 10:10). Smile, my brother. Smile, my sister. "The earth is the Lord's and the fullness there of the world, and those who dwell there in it" (Psalm 24:1).

As the story moves on, God told Balaam that Balaam could not curse what God blessed. And he couldn't curse God's people because they were blessed (Number 22:12). Friend, the enemy can't curse you once you realize that you are blessed by God the Father. Time and time again, Balak sent for Balaam to curse God's people. But each time he attempted to curse the people of God, Balaam he could not; he could only bless them. The king then sent distinguished princes, nobles, honorable men, and men of authority with at least three times as big of a reward to Balaam, but Balaam responded the same way. Balaam sent word to the king, telling him that even if he filled his palace with all the silver and gold he could find, he could only repeat what God had said about his people: They were blessed. He could not curse what God blessed.

King Balak then went with the princes of Moab to meet with their king. The king took him to various places throughout the kingdom where altars were built and sacrifices made to false gods to curse God's people. But it still would not work.

The Spirit of the Lord came upon Balaam one time as he went through the ritual of cursing the Israelites. But Balaam, instead of cursing God's people during the sacrifices to the false gods, blessed them. Balaam and the king became so enraged with Balak, and his anger burned even more. Balaam told the king, "God is not a man that he should lie, neither the son of man that he should changes his mind or repent has he not spoken, and it comes to pass, I cannot cure what God has blessed" (Numbers 23:18–20).

Finally, in the Numbers chapter 25, the Israelites were destroyed by their own doing because they refused to continue following God's precepts and his way of life. They were absorbed into the surrounding cultures. When people neglect to serve God, they will get absorbed into this world system. First Corinthians 15:33 reminds us to watch out who we associate ourselves with because bad company can and will destroy good character.

Then in Exodus 34:14–16 (AMP), we read:

> … for you shall not worship any other god; for the Lord, whose name is Jealous, is a jealous (impassioned) God [demanding what is rightfully and uniquely His]—otherwise you might make a covenant with the inhabitants of the land and they would play the prostitute with their gods and sacrifice to their gods, and someone might invite you to eat his sacrifice (meal), and you might take some of his daughters for your sons, and his daughters would play the prostitute with their gods and cause your sons also to play the prostitute (commit apostasy) with their gods [that is, abandon the true God for man-made idols].

Israelites began to worship and practice idolatry with pagan gods with their neighbors in Moab.

Because Balaam was for sale, tempted and motivated by material gain, he knew how he could help destroy the Israelites. He knew he could not curse them, but he knew that he could pull the Israelites down and destroy them. So Balaam, the false prophet, knew that if the Israelites experienced sexual immorality with the women and men of Moab, it would open the door to destroying the Israelites, their relationship with God, and their prosperity.

Afterward, Balaam introduced them to making sacrifices to other gods and the worship of Baal of Peor, the main god of the land of Moab. The Israelites committed spiritual fornication and started the practice of idolatry.

> I know where you dwell, [a place] where Satan sits enthroned. Yet you are holding fast to My name, and you did not deny My faith even in the days of Antipas, my witness, my faithful one, who was killed (martyred) among you, where Satan dwells. But I have a few things against you because you have there some [among you] who are holding to the [corrupt] teaching of Balaam, who taught Balak to put a stumbling block before the sons of Israel, [enticing them] to eat things that had been sacrificed to idols and to commit [acts of sexual] immorality. (Revelation 2:13–14 AMP)

> But I have this [charge] against you, that you tolerate the woman Jezebel, who calls herself a prophetess [claiming to be inspired], and she teaches and misleads My bondservants so that they commit [acts of sexual] immorality and eat food sacrificed to idols.

I gave her time to repent [to change her inner self and her sinful way of thinking], but she has no desire to repent of her immorality and refuses to do so. (Revelation 2:20–21 AMP)

The significant meaning of sexual immorality in these texts does not just mean for someone to be sexually involved with someone. There are several usages and meanings. The first term, *pernemi*, is a Greek word originally meant "to sell." And *pronos* refers to male prostitutes or a panderer, a symbolic use to emphasize that Israel sold out to other gods through sexual immorality. Then we have the Greek term, *porneia,* which includes all types of sexual immorality, including bestiality, adultery, extramarital sexual intercourse, pedophilia, incest, promiscuity, homosexuality, fornication, lesbianism, and premarital sex.

However, the terms "pornography" and "pornographic" come from the Greek term, *epithumeo*, meaning to lust after, set one's heart upon, long for, like in Matthew 5:28: "but I say to you that everyone who [so much as] looks at a woman with lust for her has already committed adultery with her in his heart." After being introduced to the culture of the surrounding communities, Israel began to lust after things that were not of God:

See that no one is sexually immoral, or godless like Esau, who for a single meal sold is inheritance rights, his birth rights as the oldest son. Afterwards, as you know, when he wanted to inherit this blessing, he was rejected. He could bring about no change of mind, though he sought the blessing with tears. (Hebrews 12:16–17)

The people of God began to be godless. Without the true God with whom they were in covenant, and they were now sellouts, worshipping false gods. In the act of worship, they began to call out, speak out to false gods and falsehoods. So instead of putting away the falsehood of pagan practices and the worship of other gods, they were now in covenant with them. Balaam knew that people operating in such acts would ignore the voice of God and separate themselves from God. We read in Ephesians 4:18–22 (AMP),

> For their [moral] understanding is darkened and their reasoning is clouded; [they are] alienated and self-banished from the life of God [with no share in it; this is] because of the [willful] ignorance and spiritual blindness that is [deep-seated] within them, because of the hardness and insensitivity of their heart. And they, [the ungodly in their spiritual apathy], having become callous and unfeeling, have given themselves over [as prey] to unbridled sensuality, eagerly craving the practice of every kind of impurity [that their desires may demand]. But you did not learn Christ in this way! If in fact you have [really] heard Him and have been taught by Him, just as truth is in Jesus [revealed in His life and personified in Him], that, regarding your previous way of life, you put off your old self [completely discard your former nature], which is being corrupted through deceitful desires.

They paid a heavy price. As a result of turning from what we now know as the covenant of God, twenty-four thousand of them lost their lives for being sexually immoral and worshipping and calling out to false gods.

In 1 Corinthians 6:15–20, 10:8, we also come to know and learn that the act of sexual immortality out of the confines of marriages is not just a sinful act committed against God. It is also a sinful act committed against oneself. And when you have sex with someone, you become one with that person. The bible says we become, "one flesh," with whomever we have sex with. Once we belong to God, we are his property and his temple. And in the godless act of sexual immorality, we are uniting God's temple and with an ungodly, unholy act. So Balaam knew how to destroy the people of God by drawing them out and into what they knew was punishable by death.

The children of Israel allowed themselves to be seduced and pulled out and away from God's blessings. But thanks be to God for his grace, mercy, salvation, and forgiveness of sins. Once we repent and look to God the Father in forgiveness, he can and will restore us and our rightful stances, righteousness, in him. We don't have to forfeit the blessings of the promises of God, and the promises of the covenant are still available to us. For the Word says that God has laid before us an open door of blessings or curses. The choice is ours. Which one will you choose?

CHAPTER 5

The Mind: What's on Your Mind?

1 Chronicles 28:9
Psalm 14:1
Proverbs 23:7
Isaiah 26:3
Luke 10:27
Romans 12:2
2 Corinthians 10:5
Ephesians 4:17–25
Philippians 2:5; 4:8
2 Timothy 1:7
James 1:5–8

It is God's desire that we have healthy minds, sound minds, not sick minds. We can obtain a healthy, sound mind by studying the Word of God. An old mindset versus the new mindset is our choice, I believe, through purposeful action on our part to change. God stated that he has given us a sound mind. "For God has not given us a spirit of fear, but of power and of love and of a sound mind" (2 Timothy

1:7 NKJV). Ultimately, it is God's desire that we have the mind of Christ. We all need to present the mind of Christ Jesus, in which the Word instructs us to "Let this mind be in you which was also in Christ Jesus" (Philippians 2:5 NKJV). Second Corinthians 10:5 states, "We demolish arguments and every pretension that sets itself up against the knowledge of God, and we take captive every thought to make it obedient to Christ."

Many saints do not realize or understand that it is our responsibility to take an active role in having the right mindset or the right attitude and spirit of the mind. Once we come to the knowledge of God through accepting Jesus Christ and have entered a relationship with God the Father, we must begin to take control of what comes in and stays in our minds. it is in the mind where we create, imagine, and perceive. It is in the mind where we come to know and begin to understand a thing. Everything we see has come from someone's thoughts and minds, from cookware and makeup to office supplies. Our minds are part of the realm of the soul that receives revelatory knowledge from God the Father. And it is in our minds that we first experience spiritual warfare. Why? In 2 Corinthians 10:5 (ASV), Luke said, "He answered, 'Love the Lord your God with all your heart and with all your soul and with all your strength and with all your mind' and, 'Love your neighbor as yourself.'" He's telling us to war for our minds, "casting down imaginations and every high thing that exalted itself against the knowledge of God and bringing it into captivity every thought to the obedience of Christ."

We have authority and power to take control of our thoughts. The enemy will use any and everything to attack our minds with negative and destructive thoughts and ideas. Now if we know to operate in the power and authority of God through the blood of Christ and the Word, we will have victory in our thought lives.

God has given us free will, and whether to worship him with our minds is our choice. That is why the Scriptures say let this mind be in you that was in Christ Jesus. To have the mind of Christ we must learn who he was and study and meditate on his Word. The free will of our souls do not want to learn about Christ because it takes discipline, work, and laying aside our old selves, our old ways of doing things. The enemy attacks our minds, creating a war zone to block us from worshipping God with our minds. Our mindsets can be a battleground. It is a real war with a real enemy who's fighting to kill, steal, and destroy our lives and the lives of those around us through a negative, painful, destructive mindset. Documented studies show that negative thinking can cause physical illness and release harmful chemicals into our bodies.

All of us come from a carnal life into a spirit-filled life we receive the gift of salvation by being transformed in the spirits of our minds (Romans 12:2). If our minds are changed, our actions and reactions will change. It's that simple. However, we will never see any changes if we do not allow the Word of God to transform our minds. If you change your mind, it will change your life. Learn to meditate on the Scriptures by purposely choosing to think on whatever is pure, true, and praiseworthy, as Philippians 4:8 reminds us. Actually, this scripture provides a list of what to purposely think about: "Finally, brothers and sisters, whatever is true, whatever is noble, whatever is right, whatever is pure, whatever is lovely, whatever is admirable— if anything is excellent or praiseworthy—think about such things" (Philippians 4:8).

To some folks, changing their mindsets may sound difficult. But believe me, you will have to practice taking your thoughts captive and weighing them against the Word of God. Every act of reasoning, especially major moves and life issues, should be examined through the mind of God by seeking his wisdom through reading the Word of God and prayer. James 1:5–8 (NAS) says, "But if any of you lacks wisdom, let him ask of God, who gives to all generously and without reproach, and it will be given to him. But he must ask in faith without any doubting, for the one who doubts is like the surf of the sea, driven and tossed by the wind. For that person ought not to expect that he will receive anything from the Lord, *being* a double-minded man, unstable in all his ways."

If we need to know anything, we must be truthful enough to ask our heavenly Father about it. But too often we mix the Word of God with the world's way of thinking, which causes other problems, including doubting the Word and double-mindedness. In James 1:6 (AMP), the Word tells us, "Let him ask in faith, never doubting or wavering, for he that waver or doubt is like a wave of the sea, driven by the wind and tossed back and forward. For, let that man think that he should not receive anything of the Lord." Now ask yourself why you haven't received some of your covenant blessings. Is it because one minute you may believe in the covenant and the next you don't? One minute you believe in the Word and God's system of doing things, and the next you believe in the world system of things? Which one will you choose to believe and receive from?

Basically, the verse in James is saying that double-mindedness will cause your action to be ineffective: "Be a double-minded man, unstable and restless in all his ways [in everything he thinks, feels, or decides]" (James 1:8 AMP). If someone is unstable in their thinking, they will be unstable in all their ways; and accomplish very little. They will take three steps forward to change and two and a half steps backwards, never getting anywhere. Unstable people are fickle, going from one thing to the next without completing or accomplishing anything. Fickle-minded people will not be able to flow with the change of putting off the old man and becoming new in Christ Jesus. A fickle-minded person can't flow with change; it throws them off balance in their thought processes, making it easy to lose their way quickly, forgetting who they are and who they can become. One would have to be stable with flexibility to manage change properly. So many people are not flexible in changing from old to new because they can't stay focused enough to complete or accomplish anything amid change. Fickle people are mostly confused, but the God we serve is not confused; nor is he the author of confusion. We know who's about confusion. Satan himself. God the Father said that he loves us and that he has given us a sound mind with peace (2 Timothy 1:7).

Speaking of the new man, one must begin to be renewed in the spirit of the mind if you are going to become a new person. Ephesians 4:17–24 puts it this way:

> So I tell you this, and insist on it in the Lord, that you must no longer live as the Gentiles do, in the futility of their thinking. They are darkened in their understanding and separated from the life of God because of the ignorance that is in them due to the hardening of their hearts. Having lost all sensitivity, they have given themselves over to sensuality so as to indulge in every kind of impurity, and they are full of greed. That, however, is not the way of life you learned when you heard about Christ and were taught in him in accordance with the truth that is in Jesus. You were taught, with regard to your former way of life, to put off your old self, which is being corrupted by its deceitful desires; to be made new in the attitude of your minds; and to put on the new self, created to be like God in true righteousness and holiness.

We see and come to understand that if one is going to truly become new, it must first begin in the spirit of the individual's mind because that is where all change begins. If we find ourselves not changing or becoming separated from God, it is because we have made a conscious decision not to serve God with our minds. If so, our understanding is then darkened through a voluntary ignorance. Ignorance in this verse is not because one does not know the truth. It is an ignorance that says, "I see what's before me, but I choose to think or believe otherwise." A person refusing to be renewed in the mind is someone who refuses to serve God with his or her mind. I believe the more someone ignores God, the more the person allows darkness to increase in his or her life.

In 1 Chronicles 28:9, King Solomon, one of the wisest men who ever lived, was told by his father, King David, to serve God wholeheartedly and with a willing mind because God searches the heart and understands every motive behind our thoughts. Far too many of us don't want to surrender our minds to God, but he is such a loving Father that he has given us a free will to choose what we want to do with our minds. But a mind without God is not healthy, and it has no peace. As explained in chapter 6, the heart and the mind are one in the same in the spiritual realm. "For as a man think in his heart so is he" (Proverbs 23:7 KJV). A fool said in his heart and his mind, basically meaning his soul, that there is no God. "The fool says in his heart, 'There is no God.' They are corrupt, their deeds are vile; there is no one who does good" (Psalm 14:1). Remember, in the realm of the soul, we feel, we think, and we want. So in other words, a fool does not feel there's a God, and a fool does not want or believe in God. Now that is a real fool. Foolish people do not want to acknowledge that they need to surrender their mind to God because they think they know best.

Some folks are too stubborn and proud to admit that they need a healthy mind that will give you God's peace. It is God's desire that his people have healthy minds, and we should want to have healthy minds. Take the presence of peace for instance. Thank God for his peace because a peaceful mind is the result of a healthy mind. "Thou will keep him in perfect peace whose mind is stayed on thee" (Isaiah 26:3 KJV). Now the word "perfect" in this context means to "be mature" in a thing. So this would mean perfect peace means mature peace. And having mature peace does not mean everything is calm and quiet around you. No, mature peace is a peace that does not make sense because with chaos, confusion, disorder, and other stuff had just gone insanely outrageous. But you could still have a sense of peace. The only place to obtain or get this type of peace comes from God the Father. If you are pursuing peace today, seek God, and he will give you peace. That is why some people can have peace during troubled times and bad situations; they have allowed the peace of God to come into their minds. A healthy mind is peaceful mind, and a peacefully minded person is someone who purposefully peruses and takes captive his or her thoughts, evaluating them through the Word of God. Philippians 4:8 (AMP) says, "Finally, brothers and sisters, whatever is true, whatever is noble, whatever is right, whatever is pure, whatever is lovely, whatever is admirable—if anything is excellent or praiseworthy—think about such things. Whatever you have learned or received or heard from me or seen in me—put it into practice. And the God of peace will be with you."

CHAPTER 6

The Heart: What's in Your Heart?

Psalm 51:10
Proverbs 6:16–19, 23:7
Isaiah 29:13
Matthew 22:15–18
Mark 7:2, 8
Luke 6:45
Romans 8:38
2 Corinthians 10:5
Ephesians 1:8, 3:17, 4:18
Philippians 2:5, 4:8
2 Timothy 1:7
James 1:5–8
1 Peter 2:1

In the spiritual realm the heart and the mind are two in one but are closely related in their operations and existence. However, in the natural realm they are two different body parts with two different functions. With the heart we experience emotion, feelings, we perceive and judge and come to understand things. We operate in and express love and compassion. That is why it is important to be in tune with what's in your heart. Because what we harbor in our heart will come out in our actions, reactions and even our speech; what we say out of our mouth, the heart speak. Jesus really understood the importance of this concept, knowing what's in your heart. In Luke 6:45 he states, **"A good man brings good things out of the good stored up in his heart, and an evil man brings evil things out of the evil stored up in his heart. For the mouth speaks what the heart is full of."** How does the good and evil of a person come out of them, through their speech and through their actions? A person will become what they perceive themselves to be in their heart. "As a man thinks in his heart so is he," Proverbs 23:7. Here we see the heart is referred to doing something that we associate doing with our mind, (thinking). Again, we see in Proverbs 6:16-19 the heart doing something the mind is known for, when God said that he hates a heart that devises wicked imaginations. Throughout the bible we will come to know that the heart and mind are used interchangeably. Our heart and mind are clearly and closely connected. The mind has cognitive function that helps us make decisions and understand things. Our heart functions with our emotion and feelings within the realm of the soul.

We can only be in tune with God out of the attitude of a pure heart because we serve God with our heart. The word tells that man looks on the outer appearances, but God looks at our heart. Therefore, we must strive to have a clean heart. God is concern with what's in our heart. We can fool each other and the people around us. We can pretend to be phony and fake with each other, but we cannot fool God. King David knew this and so after he had sinned, he sought the Lord and asked him in Psalms 51:10 (ESV) to, **"create in me a clean heart oh God and renew a right spirit within me."** The king had repented from his evil ways, and he had realized that we worship and serve God out a pure heart. Look what God himself had said in the book of Isaiah 29:13 "the Lord says people come near to me with their mouth and honor me with their lips, but their hearts are far from me. Their worship of me is made up only of rules taught by men." I believe God is looking for someone who will worship and serve him with a pure sincere heart. Not just following the latest style and trends in Gospel and Christian music. As we walk with the Father, we come to know that worship and worshiping God the Father is much more than music; but it is a way of life. I believe God is saying that a person with a pure heart or operating with a pure heart may not do everything right – or is a perfect person; it is the intent of their heart, wanting to love honor, and serve God. What is the intent, plan, motive, purpose in our hearts is the question? But a heart that is looking to honor, please, serve and love God in everything they do, is a pure heart.

Just like we need a healthy mind to live a victorious life we need a healthy heart to have a healthy spirit and to be a mature Christian. The Apostles Paul knew and understood this key element in his Christian development. Paul who is known to have written most of the New Testament understood the importance of being aware of what's in your heart; or should I say be conscious of the attitude of your heart. Here again we see a perfect example of God using someone who had given him a heart that was discombobulated with hatred and evil; and allowing him to clean it up with his love, compassion, and peace. Brother Paul was one who once hated Christians with a passion and murder them but when he had come to know the Lord Jesus by surrendering his heart on the Damascus Road experience in the book of Acts chapter 9, where Saul became Paul. "Saul Saul why are you persecuting me" was the question the Lord asked Paul that pricked his heart and caused him to change towards Christians. Paul had attitude of the mind / heart change, and he became a new man. Paul had an (epiphany) experience that Ephesians 1:18-19 (AMP) speak of, *"And [I pray] that the eyes of your heart [the very center and core of your being] may be enlightened [flooded with light by the Holy Spirit], so that you will know and cherish the hope [the divine guarantee, the confident expectation] to which He has called you, the riches of His glorious inheritance in the saints (God's people), and [so that you will begin to know] what the immeasurable and unlimited and surpassing greatness of His [active, spiritual] power is in us who believe."*

Now we come to learn that our heart has eyes that we may see, know, and understand God in our spiritual growth. Paul received revelation knowledge from God and spiritual insight because he was willing to acknowledge what was in his heart; and that there was something not right, he quickly repented and served God out of a pure heart. And that is the only way we too will be able to develop and grow in our faith. If our hearts are not kept clean, through repentance and what we know the spirit of God is trying to reveal to us; our understanding of the things of God will become darkened and once that happens, we then are separated and cut off from God. Once we are cut off from God, we become ignorant to the things of God and powerless in the spiritual realm. To be separated from God is death, eternal death, Hell - home of the dead, Hades, and misery on earth. Living a miserable tormented life on earth is not the will of God for any of us. Someone living like that the scriptures tells us "for their [moral] understanding is darkened *and* their reasoning is clouded; [they are] alienated *and* self-banished from the life of God [with no share in it; this is] because of the [willful] ignorance *and* spiritual blindness that is [deep-seated] within them, because of the hardness *and* insensitivity of their heart," Ephesians 4:18 (AMP) Jesus said that he came that we may have life and to have it more abundantly. We were created first to be in daily fellowship with God the Father. "For nothing can separate us from the love of God," but refusing to possess a pure heart can, Romans 8:38. So if we are separated from God, it is our choice, not God's. *So that Christ may dwell in your hearts through your faith. And may you, having been [deeply] rooted and [securely] grounded in love, Ephesians 3:17 (AMP)*, Christ Jesus desires to dwell in our hearts through faith.

Don't be a Christian with a hypocritical heart

To often we as Christians and saints don't realize that the condition of one's heart is vital to their spiritual growth and development. We must realize that there will always be spiritual growth when we are connected to a living God. Spiritual growth always aims for inner purity. True spiritual growth comes from inner purity, but our society and culture today get spiritual growth confused with promotion in the body of Christ. However, there is a difference between spiritual growth and advancing and /or promotion in the body of Christ. People can promote you, for all the wrong reasons, without spiritual growth. But true spiritual growth always has the peace of God connected to it. When promotion happens for a mature Christians, they can experience Hell, Hades all around them, but they will have and hold onto the peace of God. A person that has grown spiritually knows that the inner man is affected by what is in his / her heart, not by what's going on the outside of them. One experiencing spiritual growth aims to please God and not the crowd. They are not concern with the crowd and their traditions, their system, or ways of doing things. "And they had seen that some of His disciples ate their bread with [ceremonially] impure hands, that is, unwashed [and defiled according to Jewish religious ritual]," Mark 7:2 (AMP). When someone grows up spiritually, they know who they are in God. They realize and know that they are the righteousness of God through Christ Jesus and not because they do everything right either; but because they are connected through the covenant of God. Whenever something is not right with a person who has a pure heart, they know that they have the promise of God the Father to help them make it right. They don't profess to be one thing on the outer appearance while secretly living as someone else in their heart. In other words, they refuse to be a "hypocrite." Remember that God the Father is looking for those who will love and worship him in spirit and truth, not insincere love for him. Like Isaiah 29:13 says, people coming near him with their mouth and honor him with their lips, but their hearts are far from him. When we are not intimate and sincere with God, he rejects it because it's nothing but religious veneer, which is superficial, for show not pure / true motives and feelings. For we know that the material veneer is manmade, artificial, cheap wood, having the look of good quality wood, but it's not what it appears to be. As a matter of fact, veneer can't even handle water on it but for so long. It's not like good quality wood because it can be easily destroyed. In other words, it's not tough enough to handle harsh things and still be of good use. However, my friend a pure heart is a heart that can handle the tough things in life and still love God and others despite what's comes its way.

Anyone who is a hypocrite is a veneer person. Hypocrites are people who appear to be growing spiritually without any real change in the inner man, the heart. The outer man of a hypocrite can and may experience advancement or promotion in the body of Christ here on earth, but at the same time they are dying inwardly, with no hope or change I their heart. Hypocrites are superficial people, who pretend to be God like, but underneath there is a religious veneer, a malicious, deceitful hearted person,"_*Then the Pharisees went and conspired together plotting how to trap Him by [distorting] what He said. They sent their disciples to Him, along with the Herodians, saying, "Teacher, we know that You are sincere and that You teach the way of God truthfully, without concerning Yourself about [what] anyone [thinks or says of Your teachings]; for You are impartial and do not seek anyone's favor [and You treat all people alike, regardless of status]. Tell us then, what do You think? Is it permissible [according to Jewish law and tradition] to pay a poll-tax to Caesar, or not?" But Jesus, aware of their malice, asked, "Why are you testing Me, you hypocrites?"* Matthew 22:15-18 (AMP); but "put aside every trace of malice and all deceit and hypocrisy and envy and all slander and hateful speech," I Peter 2:1, (AMP). They display all the right religious activities, but they have a poor heart condition, a heart without the love of God. It's Always about an outer show and how things may appear to be rather than how they really are "Veneer people" with all their gifts and talents promote and advance themselves; while they aim to please the crowd, they neglect to please the very God they claim to love and serve. God so desire to change them from the inside out, but he can't unless they want to. "You have let go of the commands of God and are holding on to human traditions," Mark 7:8. Sometimes it's hard to understand how people become hypocrites or veneer people can just walk in greed, deceit, arrogance, malice, and all forms of evilness because these people have no pureness in their heart, nor are they trying have a purpose in their heart or in life in general? For some a pure heart may seem to be too difficult to have but if they were to realize that we always have the help and love of God the Father to helps us with any and everything; if they were to just call on him like King David did in Psalm 51:10 "create in me a clean heart oh God and renew a right spirit within me." King David knew that to possess a blessed life he needed to have and serve with a pure heart.

CHAPTER 7

The Mouth: What Is Coming Out of Your Mouth?

Genesis 1:1–27
Psalms 33:6; 45:1; 64:8,
Proverbs 18:21; 21:18, 23
Matthew 16:19; 22:15–18
Mark 11:13–14, 20–23
Luke 6:45; 10:19
John 10:10; 6:63–64
Romans 8:27–28
Galatians 5:20
Ephesians 4:29
2 Thessalonians 4:11
2 Timothy 3:16–17
Hebrews 4:12
James 1:26; 3:5–10
1 Peter 3:10

He who guards his mouth and his tongue
Guards himself from troubles.
Proverbs 21:23

The Scriptures are God's words that he spoke to the minds of humankind. God still speaks to his creation (men and women) through his Word. If someone wants to know what God says or how he feels, pick up his Word, the Holy Bible. We need to learn the Scriptures so that we can learn to speak the same langue as God the Father and know when he is speaking to us. In 2 Timothy 3:16–17, the Word of God tells us that "all scriptures are God breathed, (God spoken, inspired of God) and is useful for teaching, rebuking, correcting, and training in righteousness, so that the man of God may be thoroughly equipped for every good work."

Friend, the abundant life that Jesus speaks about in John 10:10 refers to some of the promises of the kingdom of God here on earth. Even though the heart and the mind are used interchangeably for spiritual growth and development, the mouth is also connected to them and vitally important for our spiritual development. Luke 6:45 states, "the [intrinsically] good man produces what is good and honorable and moral out of the good treasure [stored] in his heart; and the [intrinsically] evil man produces what is wicked and depraved out of the evil [in his heart]; for his mouth speaks from the overflow of his heart." I believe this last line speaks volumes: "For out of the overflow of his heart his mouth speaks." So many times we claim that we are waiting, hoping, and believing God to turn around a particular situation in our lives. For example, something like our finances, jobs—or the lack of—our marriages, or issues with our children. But unconsciously, we speak negatively regarding those very areas we are praying for God to turn around and make changes for the better. Try this simple exercise one day. Pay close attention to everything you speak out of your mouth. You will probably be very surprised as to how much you speak against the very thing you believed in God for. Now, once you have discovered that your talk does not really match what you believe in God for, it would seem to be easy for you to become very conscious of the things you say and to make changes in your speech. First Peter 3:10 states, "whoever would love life and see good days must keep his tongue from evil and his lips from deceitful speech." I believe this scripture has helped many of us to change our lives.

Some of us don't realize that operating under the kingdom principles of yielding our minds, hearts, and mouths to God the Father will bless our lives. We must understand that how we talk and what we say out of our mouths exposes how we truly feel deep down in our hearts, the innermost beings of our existence. Most of us want to believe that our speech is good and supports our faith in God, each other, and ourselves. But for a lot of us, this is not so. Our mouths only speak what's hidden in our hearts, and what's in our hearts was created in our minds. We must remember that there is a connection between what's in our hearts, what's on and in our minds, and what we will eventually say out of our mouths. It's so vital that we grasp this basic truth because once we began to master this truth or kingdom principles, we will begin to walk in victory in every area of our lives. We often experienced defeat because we failed to yield to practicing self-control over the mind, the heart, and the mouth. We didn't realize that all these kingdom principles affect both the spiritual realm as well as the natural realm. For the most part, some have not lived or experienced a blessed life in the earthly realm because of not making the connection of believing the principle of yielding their minds, hearts, and mouths to God. We will begin, I believe, to experience victory in every area of life by yielding them over to God the Father and practicing kingdom, spiritual principles. Then we will come to understand, know, and believe we can have an abundant life. Then and only then can we walk in wealth and health, even as our souls prosper. Or shall I say as our souls prosper, we will walk in health and wealth.

And remember that true wealth is not just about money and having things. True wealth begins in the spiritual realm. No matter what is going on around us, an abundant life is available. The truth of the matter is that we will always have issues, problems, situations, and concerns to overcome. But how we act and react regarding those problems and issues will usually determine whether we are going to live an abundant life. We must be mindful of whatever state our emotions or mindsets are in. We can be aware of what we say out of our mouths, either joyful, sad, joking, or mad. Why? Because words are spirits, active and alive (John 6:63). That's why it is important to bless and not destroy each other with our words.

All things that happen to us are not good. The enemies of daily life can sometimes even destroy and hurt us. But if we love, trust, and hope in God, he will always work things out for our good. God can turn things around for your good that were meant to destroy you. Another awesome scripture is found in Romans 8:27–28: "and he who searches our hearts knows the mind of the spirit, because the Spirit intercedes for God's people in accordance with the will of God. And we know that in all things God works for the good of those who love him, who have been called according to his purpose." When we serve God the Father, we can move from tragedy to triumph, from victim to victory. As a matter of fact, if we continue to yield our minds, hearts, and mouths to God, he can take what was designed to destroy you and use it as a major blessing for you. I believe we will experience victories in life more often if we yield and submit to God more. When some people refuse to be destroyed because of tragedy or something of that sort, they will experience blessings most times and serve as testimonies to those around them. God has given us power and authority to live in the earthly realm: "Behold I have given you power and authority to trample upon serpents and scorpions and (physical and mental strength and ability) over all the power that the enemy possesses; and nothing shall in any way harm you" (Luke 10:19). But we must remain in hope, faith, and love as we fully field our lives to God.

The Word tells us that out of the heart, the mouth speaks. If we listen to what comes out of our mouths, we will learn and understand our faith and how we truly feel. Sometimes we have not yet received what we wanted from God because we constantly destroy ourselves by what we say. Proverbs 18:21 says, "Death and life are in the power of the tongue: and they love it shall eat the fruit there of."

The power of the spoken word is how everything that exists came into being. If we were to look at the creation of life in the book of Genesis, we would see that everything God created he spoke into being. In Genesis 1:1–27, God said let there be light, and it was. God said let the water under the sky be gathered to one place and let dry ground appear. God said let the earth produce vegetation, and it did. God said let the land produce living creatures, and they came into existence. God said let us make man in our image and in our likeness and let them rule over everything that exists, and it was so. Throughout the creation story, we see that God said and then it was so. "By the word of the Lord were the Heavens made; and the entire starry host the breath of his mouth" (Psalm 33:6). God said, and God said, and whatever exists came into being.

However, in Genesis 2:7, we see that after God made man, he did not become a living being until God breathed into his nostrils the, "breath of life." The very breath we breathe is life from God. When someone speaks, he or she must breathe. You can't speak without breathing. To speak out is to breath outward. When God breathed into Adam, he spoke into Adam, and he became a living soul; God's spirit entered Adam, the first living man. And since we were created and made in God's image and likeness, we, too, have the same creative power to speak, to breathe the breath of life, a blessed and prosperous life into existence. That's why we need to be very mindful and aware of what we say and what others say to us that we agree with. We don't need to agree with everything someone says, particularly if it is not of God.

The Bible says that "all scriptures are God breathed" (2 Timothy 3:16). All words are spirit and life; scriptures are words God spoke to the minds and hearts of men. Jesus himself said in John 6:63–64, "the words I have spoken to you are spirit and they are life." In Hebrews

4:12, the word of God tells us that the "word of God is living and active, sharpen than any double-edged sword, it penetrates even to dividing the soul and spirit joints and marrow; it judges thoughts and attitudes of the heart." In other words, we have the same power to breathe life into the spiritual and natural realms of life through the words we say.

I'm not talking about the blab-it and grab-it movement we had in various religious groups starting back in the 1980s, in which people thought and believed they could just speak any and everything into existence without even agreeing with God the Father about their lives. Some folks were living any kind of way and not even honoring God, but speaking God's work without knowledge of or agreeing with his Word. Believe it or not, some people still believe and operate according to this strange doctrine without the love, knowledge, or even the acceptance of God's Word. We must remember that ultimately, God is the source of all things that are good.

Because words have power, even when we are joking around, we ought not to speak negatively or badly because they are still words coming out of our mouths. In Psalm 45:1, the Word reminds us that our tongues are the pens of skillful writers. We must learn to hold our peace and not be so quick to speak, especially when we are upset. It is likely we will later regret some of the things we said when our emotions were all out of sorts. Be slow to speak and quick to hear. The old folks used to say, "God gave us one mouth and two ears." And God's Word tells us the same thing. Proverbs 18:21 puts it this way: "The tongue has the power of life and death, and those who love it will eat its fruit." The stakes are high. Your words can either speak life or speak death. Our tongues can build others up, or they can tear them down. Too often we regret some of the things we said while upset or don't have all the information. Later on, we somehow realize that the spoken word does have power. Sometimes people are upset with what is going on and around them, but they refuse to check their speech. They refuse to take the time and responsibility to listen to what they have been really saying.

Something as simple as singing a song from the radio with negative lyrics can really affect your mind, thoughts, and eventually your life. For example, you may listen to someone singing a song because of the beat or its tune, never realizing what the lyrics really were or meant. Perhaps the song was about committing suicide. Then one day negative thoughts begin to bombard your mind and riddle your thoughts with negativity. That same person is trying to figure out from where on earth this negative mindset and suicidal feelings the individual is carrying in his or her heart are coming. Well, I tell you, my friend, they came from the fruit of the person's lips, singing and sowing the words of suicide in his or her heart and mind by singing negative songs, which appeared harmless at the time. For some people, it would never occur to them that they need to stop singing certain songs because our actions come from our thoughts, and our thoughts come from what is sown in our hearts. Therefore, our minds and hearts are closely related.

Remember we were created in the image and likeness of God our Father, so we have that same creative power as God, who spoke everything into existence. Still not convinced that our lives are affected by what we say? Let's look at two scriptures: "I will give you the keys of the kingdom of heaven; whatever you bind on earth will be bound in heaven, and whatever you loose on earth will be loosed in heaven" (Matthew 16:19). "I have given you authority to trample on snakes and scorpions and to overcome all the power of the enemy; nothing will harm you" (Luke 10:19). God has said that he has given us the keys of the kingdom by declaring and speaking to situations and circumstances in our lives. Not only do we have the keys to speak to our world, we also have the authority and power to change our world through what we say. Some folks can speak to things all day long, but without the authority, power, and help of God to change things, nothing will ever happen because heaven is not backing them up. But hallelujah and glory to God that heaven is backing us up. Thanks be to God, who has given us power and authority to speak in faith and his name to create change in this world for the better. In Mark

11:13–14, 20–23, Jesus demonstrates the same ability to change his world by speaking to it when he spoke to the fig tree that had no fruit.

The Misuse of Our Mouths: Verbal Abuse

In the same sense, the tongue is a small part of the body, and yet it boasts of great things. See [by comparison] how great a forest is set on fire by a small spark! And the tongue is [in a sense] a fire, the very world of injustice and unrighteousness; the tongue is set among our members as that which contaminates the entire body and sets on fire the course of our life [the cycle of man's existence] and is itself set on fire by Hell (Gehenna). For every species of beasts and birds, of reptiles and sea creatures, is tamed and has been tamed by humanity. But no one can tame the human tongue; it is a restless evil [undisciplined, unstable], full of deadly poison. With it we bless our Lord and Father, and with it we curse men, who have been made in the likeness of God. Out of the same mouth come both blessing and cursing. These things, my brothers, should not be this way [for we have a moral obligation to speak in a manner that reflects our fear of God and profound respect for His precepts]. (James 3:5–10 AMP)

The misuse of our mouths has caused us and others so much pain, hurt, and suffering. Simply saying and talking about the wrong things can be harmful and destructive to our spiritual and physical lives. Unnecessary problems, trouble, and confusion have come in to our lives because of not exercising discipline and authority in the area of what comes out our mouths. Too often we take no thought as to what comes out of our mouths, so we commit various sins of the mouth. Sins of the mouth are just as bad as any other sin. But what is disturbing is that most of us don't seem to think so or realize it. Life and death are in the power of our tongues (Proverbs 18:21).

Take, for example, verbal abuse. It is just as harmful as physical abuse, but few people seem to be paying attention to that fact. We can see the markings of physical abuse; it is hard to hide. However, verbal abuse may not mark the body or leave lasting physical scars and marks. But it does leave lasting marks and scars on one's heart, spirit, and mind. And if the abuse is allowed to go on, it can cause deep wounds in one's spirit and soul. Satan, the devil himself, really knows this simple truth. That is why he uses verbal abuse to kill, steal, and destroy a person's life. Anybody who has yielded himself or herself to the spirit of verbal abuse is under demonic influence, sometimes without ever realizing it. Therefore, the Word says get rid of fits of rage (Galatians 5:20). "Do not let any unwholesome talk come out of your mouths, but only what is helpful for building others up according to their needs, that it may benefit those who listen" (Ephesians 4:29). But being under demonic influence does not have to be your yoke of bondage. We can repent, turn back to God, ask for his forgiveness, and begin to live in peace again.

Normally, we cannot see evidence of verbal abuse with our eyes. But if we look at the one's spirit and listen with our hearts, we can tell if a person has been abused or is an abuser. Most people who suffer from something like low self-esteem, I believe, have been verbally abused at one time or another. Because of the craftiness of the enemy, some folks have been verbally abused and others verbal abusers and don't even realize they have been or are being used by the enemy.

In fact, some verbal abusers are so crafty you may not be aware that you were being abused until years after it happened. Someone who is being discouraging, humiliating, harsh, rude, or condescending, but with a nice tone of voice, can be just as abusive as someone who yells and curses. I believe it is the words, the spirit, and the intent of the heart behind what someone says that make it abuse—the words they use, the spirit in which they are said, and the intention of one's heart. It is my belief that some abusers don't know what's going with themselves; perhaps they are out of touch with reality. Therefore, they may have spoken in a negative and destructive manner for so long that verbal abuse is normal to them. Any form of abuse is all that some people know. But abuse, verbal or physical, is demonic.

There are major signs of an abusive person. For one, they may have a false sense of humility. At first glance, this type of person may appear to be very humble and peaceful, but that will soon change and blow his or her cover when things don't go that individual's way. Rude, nasty, critical, negative, sharp, and abrupt people are normally verbally abusive when they are upset. During times like that, it is difficult for them to hide who they really are.

Verbally abusive people come from all walks of life. Unfortunately, many are in authoritative positions, such as a parent, supervisor, minister, or law enforcement. Verbal abusers believe they have the right to talk anyway they want to anybody. Most verbal abusers have been abused at some point in their lives, or they are currently being abused. Unfortunately, verbal abuse is a vicious circle that goes on and on, until someone is willing to acknowledge it, expose it, and refuse to let it continue any longer.

Although verbal abuse can be settled at times, it still needs to be addressed. A verbally abusive person needs to be constantly confronted, I believe the truth of God's Word that their behavior is unacceptable and must not be tolerated: "Do not let any unwholesome talk come out of your mouths, but only what is helpful for building others up according to their needs, that it may benefit those who listen" (Ephesians 4:29).

Believe it or not, many of us have the markings of someone who has been verbally abused or we know someone who is an abuser. One time or another, most of us have been on both sides of the spectrum of an abuser, though maybe not as extreme as some. I believe all of us have been affected by the issues of verbal abuse. Just because verbal abuse is widespread in our society, it does not give anyone the right to do it. And please, never accept it because it is demonic. If you ever want to see Satan in human form, just look at someone who is verbally abusive, and you will see demonic activity in action.

However, children of God have nothing to fear because we have authority over that spirit. And that is just what verbal abuse is—an evil spirit that speaks. And we have power to rebuke it by speaking the, "Blood of Jesus," against it. In Jesus's name, Amen. Believers need to realize that they have power over all the works of the devil through the proper use of our mouths. By speaking God's Word against all the enemy's works and believing what we say in the name of Jesus, it is promised to us that we shall have victory in every area of our lives. This is another privilege we have as part of God's kingdom, pleading the blood of Jesus Christ and speaking God's Word in faith against demonic forces.

The Curse of a Gossiper

First Peter 3:10 says, "Whoever would love life and see good days must keep their tongue from evil and their lips from deceitful speech."

> Do not let any unwholesome talk come out of your mouths, but only what is helpful for building others up according to their needs, that it may benefit those who listen. And do not grieve the Holy Spirit of God, with whom you were sealed for the day of redemption. (Ephesians 4:29–30)

Friend, some of us have not experienced a blessed life or the promises of the kingdom because we have refused to yield our mouths to the authority of God's Word. Not speaking well of others and oneself, I believe, is gossip and verbal abusive. Again, it is important to bless people with our words. We must begin to take authority over our flesh—which is the old person, our natural person—and practice self-control over what comes out of our mouths concerning others and ourselves. One day we will have to account for every word that comes out of our mouths. What we speak out of our mouths affects every area of our lives, kingdom people or not. Either we are a blessing with our mouths, or we are cursing with it. I ask you, which one are you doing on a regular basis toward others and self, cursing or blessing? Before you answer, remember we always reap what we sow. Some of us are holding up our own blessings, breakthroughs, miracles, and even the promises of the kingdom simply because we refuse to acknowledge we suffer from the loose-lip syndrome, speaking every negative thing that comes to mind. We must grow up and mature in the spirit and realize that the enemy attacks our minds with negative, destructive thoughts he wants you to speak against yourself because he can't stop you. You stop you by the things you speak. From time to time, we may have said negative, destructive words out of our mouths about people. Not only can we stop or hold up the flow of blessings from coming into our lives by what we say, we also grieve the Holy Spirit that dwells inside us by gossiping and saying things that do not glorify God. If we are grieving the Spirit of God, we can't feel well or have peace because the Holy Spirit is the actual presence of God that gives us peace and reassurance that he is inside us. No one in his or her right mind would ever want to sadden the Holy Spirit because the Holy Spirit gives us the wisdom, knowledge, understanding, and joy of God. And the joy of the Lord is our strength. We need the strength of the Lord to live in this world. Without any price to us, Jesus left the Holy Spirit with us to lead and guide us into all truth with peace and joy.

Do you remember the old joke or phrase, "Loose lips sink ships"? The phrase originated in the United States during World War II as part of a propaganda campaign. Though it was part of the war effort, most of us probably did not realize that it was true when it came to words from our mouths. This joke, phrase also became famous by an African American comedian- actor known by the name of Flip Wilson in the early 1970s. But the Word of God still makes it plain and simple of the importance of being aware and control what we speak out of our mouths. "If anyone consider himself religious and yet does not keep a tight rein on his tongue, he deceives himself and his religion is worthless. The religion of a man that God our Father accepts as pure and faultless is knowing how to bridle one's tongue. Those who consider themselves religious and yet do not keep a tight rein on their tongues deceive themselves, and their religion is worthless" (James 1:26).

For too often, we are taught that murder, adultery, and sins of that sort are bad. And they are. But we say people who commit such things have issues and no morals or principles. But according to the Word of God, a gossiper is just as bad. We have neglected to realize that sin is sin in the eyes of a holy, righteous God; sin is bad no matter what. When we don't line up with the Word, we will always judge ourselves according to each other's standard instead of aligning with the grace of God. Therefore, we become the righteousness of God because of his grace, not of our own strength and abilities. We could never stand based on our abilities alone. It is by the grace of God that we're able to live lives of faith for we can do nothing without him.

Sins of the mouth are just as bad as murder in the eyes of a Holy God because both can destroy someone's life. There are no big sins and little sins. Many lives have been destroyed and ripped apart due to the slip of the tongue or loose lips. Some have purposely tried to destroy the lives of others by what they have said. Slander, lies, rumors, or perhaps sharing something that ought not be shared have hurt a lot of folks. Therefore, it is very important to be mindful and to use caution about what comes out of our mouths, especially when we are angry, upset, sick, or depressed. What comes out of our mouths can directly affect us. First Peter 3:10 reminds us that any and every kind of thing out of our mouths can hinder, stop, block, and destroy our lives, our prosperity, and our blessings. Not only can sins of the mouth destroy our lives, they can also destroy the lives of those around us and those who love to listen to all who are called gossipers and whispers. Psalm

59:12 says, "For the sins of their mouths, for the words of their lips, let them be caught in their pride. For the curses and lies they utter."

Whispers are what the Bible calls a gossiping person with a malicious tongue who has destroyed many lives. Some people really have a gossiping problem. They gossip so much, they even gossip about themselves, not even realizing it. The god of this world has blinded their minds, and they can't understand the effects of talking too much about the wrong things, which is downright wicked. Some have forgotten their whole lives are about reaping and sowing. We reap what we have sown. When we gossip and sow seeds of slander to destroy someone, or just spread poison about someone, it can and will come back to you. "Their own tongues will ruin them, and all who see them will shake their heads in scorn" (Psalm 64:8 NLT).

Even taking part in such things we know are not good releases poison in one's spirit. When we know someone is a gossiper and consistently listen to them, we are receptive to the poison they spew into our spirits, contaminating us with their poison. Poison is designed to kill and destroy. The poison of a gossiper will always kill and destroy the lives of others. Who do we know that comes into people's lives to kill, steal, and destroy? The thief, Satan. We read in John 10:10, "The thief comes only to steal and kill and destroy; I have come that they may have life and have it to the full." God's Word tells us to guard our hearts and minds because out of it flows the issues of life. Stop listening to the poison of a gossiper because it is designed to destroy you. Most gossipers shares gossip about someone with you will gossip about you as soon as they get a chance. Most gossipers are critical people who sit in judgment of others. And the Word says do not judge lest you will be judged by the same measure. And we are not the lawgiver; there is only one.

People who are critical of others are usually ashamed or have hidden fears, weaknesses, or problems they are trying to cover up. Most gossipers have low self-esteem. They really don't like who they are, so they constantly compare themselves with others instead of sizing themselves up with the Word of God and letting the mind of Christ dwell in them and do something new in them. In 2 Thessalonians 3:11, the Word calls these types of people busybodies, jealous and envious people who really need to get their own lives and stay out of other people's business. "Make it your goal to live a quiet life, minding your own business and working with your hands, just as we instructed you before" (1 Thessalonians 4:11).

Stop Griping

> These people are grumblers and faultfinders; they follow their own evil desires; they boast about themselves and flatter others for their own advantage. (Jude 1:26)

The Word says grumblers and complainers, walking according to their own lusts, have their mouths full of great swelling words, and they flatter people just to get an advantage. If people knew or understood that complaining, murmuring, and grumbling can stop, hold up, and block blessings from flowing into their lives, they would do less of it. There are so many reasons why God hates a complaining, grumbling spirit. One reason is because it's negative and brings an element of division, rebellion, and discord with God, others, and even with oneself. Remember that God is the Father of unity and harmonizing. A person who has a grumbling and complaining spirit displays discontentment with life. So, for one to be discontented with the gift of life that God gave him or her is to express doubt that God the Father can bless one's life.

Another reason God hates a murmuring, grumbling, and complaining spirit is because it is annoying and disruptive. Praise and worship are good, sound good, and bless the souls of those who hear it. We know that praise and worship can bring healing to some and even usher one into the presences of God. However, being disruptive and annoying usher you into depression, frustration, anger, and the presence of Satan, just to name a few. God inhabits the praises of his people. God does not inhabit the complaining, grumbling, annoying, and disruptive because they do not glorify or honor him, like praising does. Rather, they are examples of contaminated praise, which glorifies Satan.

In other words, look at faith and fear. Fear is contaminated faith, and it is not of God. Nor does it honor him. We honor God with our faith because he gave it to us to operate in; nor did he give us fear. Second Timothy 1:7 (NKJV) says, "For God has not given us a spirit of fear, but of power and of love and of a sound mind."

Since God the Father didn't give us the spirit of fear, I don't honor him when I walk in fear. What fear is to Satan is what faith is to God. And what grumbling is to Satan, praise is to God. So who are you blessing, glorifying with your mouth? Murmurs don't have peace in their souls or lives because what's in a person's heart will eventually come out of their mouths; "Guard your heart above all else, for it determines the course of your life" (Proverbs 4:23). Just think about someone who constantly complains about any and everything. It is like poison from their lips. And if you listen to it long enough and you allow it to get into your spirit, it will affect you. But praise and the joy of God uplift your spirit and whoever hears it, allowing it inside them. Just as praise and joy uplifts you, constant complaining will take you down. I believe it also opens the door to demonic activity. So walk in victory in every area of your life, and give God the glory in your mind, your heart, and with your month.

> And don't grumble as some of them did, and then were destroyed by the angel of death. (1 Corinthians 10:10 NLT)

> Therefore, my beloved, as you have always obeyed, not as in my presence only, but now much more in

my absence, work out your own salvation with fear and trembling; for it is God who works in you both to will and to do for His good pleasure. Do all things without complaining and disputing, that you may become blameless and harmless, children of God without fault in the midst of a crooked and perverse generation, among whom you shine as lights in the world, holding fast the word of life, so that I may rejoice in the day of Christ that I have not run in vain or labored in vain. (Philippians 2:14 NKJ)

Yet you were not willing to go up [to take possession of it] but rebelled against the command of the Lord your God. You murmured and were ill-tempered (discontented) in your tents, and said, "Because the Lord hates us, He has brought us from the land of Egypt to hand us over to the Amorites to destroy us. Where can we go up? Our brothers (spies) have made our hearts melt [in fear] and demoralized us by saying, 'The people are bigger and taller than we; the cities are large and fortified [all the way up] to heaven. And besides, we saw the [giant-like] sons of the Anakim there.' Then I said to you, "Do not be shocked, nor fear them. The Lord your God who goes before you will fight for you Himself, just as He did for you in Egypt before your [very] eyes, and in the wilderness where you saw how the Lord your God carried and protected you, just as a man carries his son, all along the way which you traveled until you arrived at this place." Yet in spite of this word, you did not trust [that is, confidently rely on and believe] the Lord your God, who went before you along the way, in fire by night and in a cloud by day, to seek a place for you to make camp and to show you the way in which you should go. (Deuteronomy 1:26-33)

And the Lord heard the sound of your words, and He was angry and took an oath, saying, "Not one of these men, this evil generation, shall see the good land which I swore (solemnly promised) to give to your fathers, except Caleb the son of Jephunneh; he shall see it, and to him and to his children I will give the land on which he has walked, because he has followed the Lord completely [and remained true to Him]." (Deuteronomy 1:26–36 AMP)

Then they despised the pleasant land; they did not believe His word, but complained in their tents, and did not heed the voice of the Lord. Therefore, He raised His hand in an oath against them, to overthrow them in the wilderness. (Psalm 106:25–26 NKJV)

Scriptures That Help with Taking Control and Authority of Your Mouth

Whoever would love life and see good days must keep their tongue from evil and their lips from deceitful speech. (1 Peter 3:10)

Proverbs 26:20-28

Without wood a fire goes out; without a gossip a quarrel dies down. As charcoal to embers and as wood to fire, so is a quarrelsome person for kindling strife. The words of a gossip are like choice morsels; they go down to the inmost parts. Like a coating of silver dross on earthenware are fervent lips with an evil heart. Enemies disguise themselves with their lips, but in their hearts, they harbor deceit. Though their speech is charming, do not believe them, for seven abominations fill their hearts. Their malice may be concealed by deception, but their wickedness will be exposed in the assembly. Whoever digs a pit will fall into it; if someone rolls a stone, it will roll back on them. A lying tongue hates those it hurts, and a flattering mouth works ruin. (Proverbs 26:20–28)

The wise in heart are called discerning, and gracious words promote instruction. Prudence is a fountain of life to the prudent, but folly brings punishment to fools. The hearts of the wise make their mouths prudent, and their lips promote instruction. Gracious words are a honeycomb, sweet to the soul and healing to the bones. (Proverbs 16:21–24)

The words of the mouth are deep waters, but the fountain of wisdom is a rushing stream. It is not good to be partial to the wicked and so deprive the innocent of justice. The lips of fools bring them strife, and their mouths invite a beating. The mouths of fools are their undoing, and their lips are a snare to their very lives. The words of a gossip are like choice morsels; they go down to the inmost parts. (Proverbs 18:4–8)

The tongue has the power of life and death, and those who love it will eat its fruit. (Proverbs 18:21)

The tongue of the righteous is choice silver, but the heart of the wicked is of little value. The lips of the righteous nourish many, but fools die for lack of sense. (Proverbs 10:20–21)

From the mouth of the righteous comes the fruit of wisdom, but a perverse tongue will be silenced. The lips of the righteous know what finds favor, but the mouth of the wicked only what is perverse. (Proverbs 10:31–32)

A good man brings good things out of the good stored up in his heart, and an evil man brings evil things out of the evil stored up in his heart. For the mouth speaks what the heart is full of. (Luke 6:45)

Do not let any unwholesome talk come out of your mouths, but only what is helpful for building others up according to their needs, that it may benefit those who listen. And do not grieve the Holy Spirit of God, with whom you were sealed for the day of redemption. (Ephesians 4:29–30)

But no human being can tame the tongue. It is a restless evil, full of deadly poison. With the tongue we praise our Lord and Father, and with it we curse human beings, who have been made in God's likeness. (James 3:8–9)

For the sins of their mouths, for the words of their lips, let them be caught in their pride. For the curses and lies they utter, consume them in your wrath consume them till they are no more. (Psalm 59:12–13)

CHAPTER 8

God's Promises: A Divine Assurance of a Blessed Life

Isaiah 1:19–20
Proverbs 3:21–22; 8:17–21; 10:22; 14:1
Matthew 4:1–4
Mark 10:28–30
Luke 1:37–38
John 1:1–14; 10:3–5, 10
1 Thessalonians 2:13
Hebrews 4:12
James 1:21
3 John 1:2

God the Father really has an abundant life for us to live, which he tells us so many times. Proverbs 8:17–21 (AMP) reinforces this truth: "Wealth and glory accompany me—substantial honor and a good name. My benefits are worth more than a big salary, even a very large salary; the returns on me exceed any imaginable bonus you can find me on the righteous road—that's where I walk, at the intersection of Justice Avenue handing out life to those who love me, filling their arms with life—armloads of life." One of the most important things Proverbs 8: 17-21 should remind us of is that wealth is not just about having a lot of money and material things. True wealth is about having a prosperous spirit, life, and enjoying and loving the life you have been giving. Also knowing, loving, and being grateful to God the Father for the life he has given you, or shall I say, gifted you. John 10:10 tells us that Jesus stated, "the thief comes only to steal and kill and destroy; I have come that they may have life and have it to the full."

Third John 1:2 (AMP) describes it for us: "Beloved I pray that you may prosper in every way and (that your body) may keep well, even as (I know) your soul keeps well and prospers." Now that is living a blessed life on purpose. "For the word of God is alive and active and sharper than any two-edged sword and piercing as far as the division of soul and spirit of both joints and marrow and able to judge the thoughts and intentions of the heart" (Hebrews 4:12 AMP).

True Wealth and Riches: Wisdom, a Pathway to Wealth

Material prosperity is temporary wealth. True wealth that comes from the wisdom of God's Word is, however, enduring and lasting. The richness of wisdom is more precious and valuable than any treasures. But one who lives a godly life through his Word will have material prosperity with peace. Material prosperity and wealth without peace is not good. "The blessing of the Lord brings wealth, without painful toil for it" (Proverbs 10:22).

> I love those who love me; And those who diligently seek me will find me. Riches and honor are with me. Enduring wealth and righteousness. My fruit is better than gold, even pure gold, And my yield *better* than choicest silver. I walk in the way of righteousness. In

the midst of the paths of justice, to endow those who love me with wealth, That I may fill their treasuries. (Proverbs 8:17–21)

There are certain things I believe we can take part in that lead us toward the ability to live a blessed life. With these things we position ourselves to be blessed. As we just read, walking in love toward God, God the Father, said clearly that he loves those who love him and blesses them with riches (Proverbs 8:17–21). Along with that, obedience to the voice of God speaks to us from his Word, walking in the wisdom of God that we get from leaning and studying his Word. Not only does walking in obedience, love, and wisdom, acknowledging God, honoring and praising him, and being thankful and grateful to him will lead one to a blessed life, a prosperous life, that is promised to us.

> "Come now, let us reason together," says the Lord. "Though your sins are like scarlet, they will be as white as snow; though they are as red as crimson, they will become like wool. If you are willing and obedient, you will eat the best of the land. But if you resist and rebel, you will be devoured by the sword." For the mouth of the Lord has spoken. (Isaiah 1:19–20)

> Peter began to say to Him, "Look, we have left everything and followed You." "Truly I tell you," Jesus replied, "no one who has left home or brothers or sisters or mother or father or children or fields for My sake and for the gospel will fail to receive a hundredfold in the present age—houses and brothers and sisters and mothers and children and fields, along with persecutions—and in the age to come, eternal life. (Mark 10:28–30)

Wisdom has led me to a blessed life and wealth that no amount of money can be buy comes from knowing God's Word for yourself. This type of wealth and richness of soul has the peace of God with it. "My son, let them not vanish from your sight; Keep sound wisdom and discretion, so they will be life to your soul; And adornment to your neck" (Proverbs 3:21–22). There is nothing wrong with having monetary wealth, but monetary wealth is not the only way to have a blessed life; but it can include monetary wealth. Having financial security in this life is a good thing and a blessing as well. However, there comes a time in life when you need the peace, wisdom, and the power of God in your life. I have learned that these things can only come from knowing God's Word. Having such things as peace, wisdom, and God's power puts you in a position of living a blessed life. These types of attributes, I believe, will not only bless you and your life but those around you. Saturating oneself with God's Word can open you to hearing the voice of God. Being led and guided by God's voice through his Word, I believe, is being led by God's spirit, the Holy Spirit. To be led by the Holy Spirit will always lead to a blessed life. The Bible tells us that the Holy Spirit will lead and guide you to all truths. Now that is putting oneself in a position to be blessed!

Living a life that is blessed of God and man with God's peace is a good. This means we have a part to play in this. Knowing God's voice through his Word is up to us. We are reminded in John 10:3–5 that God's children will not follow the voice of a stranger because they know God's voice. Foolish people are arrogant and proud; they don't look to God or his Word. But a humble heart, yielding to God's Word, will lead to a life of wealth beyond measure, eternal wealth that will never lose. "For the director of music. Of David. The fool says in his heart, 'There is no God.' They are corrupt, their deeds are vile; there is no one who does good" (Proverbs 14:1).

Evil behavior will not submit to God or the authority of his Word. "Therefore, get rid of all moral filth and the evil that is so prevalent and humbly accept the word planted in you, which can save you" (James 1:21). First Thessalonians 2:13 tell us, "And we also thank God continually because, when you received the word of God, which you heard from us, you accepted it not as a human word, but as it actually is, the word of God, which is indeed at work in you who believe."

While going through his wilderness experience, being tested and tried, Jesus was faced with wondering if he trusted God the Father's Word or to believe what he saw and was going through. At that moment he had to choose to believe the Father at his Word during a hard time. There will come a time in this life when we will be faced with a decision to trust the father at his Word or to believe what you see. The moment Satan confronted Jesus in the wilderness with doubt and unbelief, Jesus stood his ground and told Satan that "man does not live by bread alone, but by ever word that comes out of the mouth of God" (Matthew 4:4).

> Then Jesus was led up by the Spirit into the wilderness to be tempted by the devil. And after He had fasted forty days and forty nights, He then became hungry. And the tempter came and said to Him, "If You are the Son of God, command that these stones become bread." But He answered and said, "It is written, 'Man shall not live on bread alone, but on every word that proceeds out of the mouth of God.'" (Matthew 4:1–4)

Terms to Learn and Know

Logos—God expressed word, revealed knowledge of God, logic, and the logic and understanding of the Word.

Rhema—God's powerful, operative spoken word.

Phone—God's breathed word, inspired written Word, Scriptures, or authoritative scriptures.

The Word took on human form and came to dwell among us. The term "word" is translated in Greek as "Rhema and Logos." Rhema means spoken word. Take, for instance, when the angel of the Lord spoke to Mary, Jesus's mother, about his conception. The message of God to Mary was spoken to her by the angel of God known as Gabriel. The angel told Mary about the child she would conceive, and Mary responded, "let it be according to thy word" (Luke 1:37–38). The other meaning of the term "word" is "Logos," meaning the divine Word or reason incarnate in Jesus Christ. John1:1–14 tells us,

> In the beginning was the Word, and the Word was with God, and the Word was God. He was in the beginning with God. All things came into being through Him, and apart from Him nothing came into being that has come into being. In Him was life, and the life was the Light of men. The Light shines in the darkness, and the darkness did not comprehend it. There came a man sent from God, whose name was John. He came as a witness, to testify about the Light, so that all might believe through him. He was not the Light, but he came to testify about the Light. There was the true Light which, coming into the world, enlightens every man. He was in the world, and the world was made through Him, and the world did not know Him. He came to His own, and those who were His own did not receive Him. But as many as received Him, to them He gave the right to become children of God, even to those who believe in His name, who were born, not of blood nor of the will of the flesh nor of the will of man, but of God. And the Word became flesh, and dwelt among us, and we saw His glory, glory as of the only begotten from the Father, full of grace and truth.

The Divine Word, the second person of the Trinity incarnate in the person of Jesus, is a Spirit, the message of truth. God's Word became flesh; took on human form, and dwelt among us. We have a God who became flesh so he could be our high priest, who is able to empathize with our weaknesses, tempted in every way just as we are, but the Word, Jesus, did not sin. Jesus was the word that became flesh and dwelt among us so we could become living epistles, the living Word. and dwelt among people. We read in 2 Corinthians 3:2–3, "You yourselves are our letter, written on our hearts, known, and read by everyone. You show that you are a letter from Christ, the result of our ministry, written not with ink but with the Spirit of the living God, not on tablets of stone but on tablets of human hearts."

Following are some other scriptures that speak life to one's soul and helps us to understand the importance of God's Word in the development of our new lives—a spiritual life and a prosperous, blessed life.

> Walk in obedience to all that the Lord your God has commanded you, so that you may live and prosper and prolong your days in the land that you will possess. (Deuteronomy 5:33)

> This is my comfort and consolation in my affliction that your word has revived me and given me life. (Psalm 119:50 AMP)

Your word is a lamp to my feet and a light to my path. (Psalm 119:105)

> I have hidden your word in my heart that I might not sin against you. With my lips I recount all the laws that come from your mouth. (Psalm 119:11–13)

> My son pay attention to what I say, listen closely to my words. Do not let them out of your sight keep

them within your heart; for they are life to those who find them and health to a man's whole body. (Proverbs 4:20–22)

So is my word that goes out from my mouth; it will not return to me empty but will accomplish what I desire and achieve the purpose for which I sent it. (Isaiah 55:11)

For you have been born again not of seed, which is perishable, but imperishable, that is through the living and abiding word of God. (1 Peter 1:23)

Praise the Lord. Blessed are those who fear the Lord, who find great delight in his commands. Their children will be mighty in the land; the generation of the upright will be blessed. Wealth and riches are in their houses, and their righteousness endures forever. Even in darkness light dawns for the upright, for those who are gracious and compassionate and righteous. Good will come to those who are generous and lend freely, who conduct their affairs with justice. Surely the righteous will never be shaken; they will be remembered forever. They will have no fear of bad news; their hearts are steadfast, trusting in the Lord. Their hearts are secure, they will have no fear; in the end they will look in triumph on their foes. They have freely scattered their gifts to the poor, their righteousness endures forever; their horn will be lifted high in honor. The wicked will see and be vexed, they will gnash their teeth and waste away; the longings of the wicked will come to nothing. Psalm 112:1-10 (NIV)

PRAYER AND INSTRUCTION
FOR A REDEEMED LIFE

Dear friend, to possess the kingdom of God here on earth and be in covenant with God the Father; one must first come to know and understand their heavenly Father through a personal relationship with him and his Son, Jesus Christ. The only way one can have this relationship is by accepting Jesus Christ as his or her personal Lord and Savior. You can do this by first believing that Jesus Christ is Lord. Then confess your sins and purposely turn from a lifestyle of sin, death, and damnation. You can surrender your life to God by praying this simple prayer and allowing him to fill your heart with the His Holy Spirit.

> Father in the name of Jesus, I recognize and acknowledge that I am a sinner. I now repent and purposely turn from a life of sin, death, and destruction. I confess with my mouth and believe in my heart that Jesus Christ is Lord and that you raised him from the dead. I invite you Lord Jesus to come into my heart and into my life and fill me with your Holy Spirit and with your love. Thank you, Lord; for saving me Amen. (Romans 10:9–10)

Welcome to the family of God. Ephesians 2:19 tell us that we are, "no longer foreigners and aliens, but fellow citizens with God's people and members of God's household." Now that you have prayed and confessed, I pray that you will follow these simple instruction to develop a strong spiritual life:

> Pray study and obey God's word daily. Be joyful and purposely walk in love. (2 Timothy 3:16; 1 Thessalonians 5:16–18)

> Find a good Bible-believing church and join. Be faithful and committed in a local church. Don't let anything or anyone turn you back. (Hebrews 10:25)

> Get baptized by water. (Matthew 3:6)

> Pray and ask the Holy Spirit to baptize in the spirit with the evidence of speaking in tongues. (Acts 2:3–4)

> Remember that God's love will never fail you. (John 3:16; 2 Corinthians 13:8)

If you fall in your daily walk with God, remember his love, get up, repent by purposely turning away from sin, and keep on walking with God.

PRAYER OF AGREEMENT

Hallelujah! Thank you, Father, for everything. You are great, almighty, wonderful, and breathtaking. I love you. I praise you, and I honor you. Today, Lord, forgive me for not believing and trusting your direction, wisdom, and guidance. I renounce the spirits of fear, doubt, and unbelief. Father, cause my very thoughts to agree with your will and purpose for my life. Help me to know, learn, and operate in your divine will for my life. Where I am weak, Lord, help me to lean on, trust, and operate in your strength. Where I am strong, show me how to be a blessing to others and neither haughty nor arrogant. May my life always bring you glory. In the mighty name of Jesus, Amen.

BIBLIOGRAPHY

Augustusel, Vernadette R. *What Does Love Have to Do with It? Understanding and Operating in the Power of God.* WestBow Press, April 2021.

Augustusel, Vernadette R. *Being Committed in a Difficult Place.* WestBow Press, June 2020.

Augustusel, Vernadette R. *Don't Worry Worship, Worship Don't Worry.* WestBow Press, June 2017.

Bowden, John, Alan Richardson, eds. *The Westminster Dictionary of Christian Theology.* Philadelphia: The Westminster Press, 1983.

Evangelical Dictionary of Biblical Theology. Grand Rapids: Banker Book House Co., 1996.

Webster's II New College Dictionary. Houghton Mifflin Co. 1995.

Biblical References

Old Testament Hebrew Lexicon, http://www.Studylight.org.
New Testament Greek Lexicon, http://www.Studylight.org.
Old Testament, https://www.biblegateway.com.
New Testament, https://www.biblegateway.com.
Old Testament, https://www.biblehub.com.
New Testament, https://www.biblehub.com.

Printed in the United States
by Baker & Taylor Publisher Services